MUTUAL

FUNDS

Comprehensive Beginner's Guide
to create Wealth using Mutual Funds

Table of Contents

Introduction 1

   The ground rules of mutual fund investing.............................. 3

Chapter 1: Understanding Mutual Funds...................................... 9

   The Structure of Mutual Funds 11

   Classes of Mutual Funds... 13

   How Mutual Funds Work 14

   Characteristics of a Mutual Fund 14

   Net Asset Value of a Mutual Fund 15

   Advantages of Investing in Mutual Funds.............................. 15

   Disadvantages of Investing in Mutual Funds 18

   How to set and manage your investment goals 21

   Safety of money in mutual funds:....................................... 26

Chapter 2: Types of Mutual Funds.......................................29

   Mutual Funds Based on Bonds 30

Mutual Funds Based on Money Market Assets or Securities.....32

Mutual Funds Based on Equities or Stocks..................................33

Income Funds...35

Balanced Funds 37

Equity Funds..38

ELSS: 40

Benefits of ELSS: 40

Global Funds 42

Specialty Funds 43

Mutual Insurance..45

Index Funds...46

Factors to consider up when setting up an investment plan..47

How to manage your investment...50

Chapter 3: Top Mistakes to Avoid When Venturing in Mutual Funds 53

Avoid going for the wrong managers.......................................54

Choosing the Right Fund Manager...54

The prospectus..55

Important Information in The Prospectus 55

Chapter 4: How to Select A Mutual Fund 65

Avoiding Loads and High Expenses 72

Best Fund Companies...74

Turnover and Taxes..76

Dangers associated with market timing...................................77

Chapter 5: The Buying and Selling Process of Mutual Fund Shares **79**

Exchange of Mutual Fund Shares 81

How an Investor Earns from Mutual Funds 81

Fees and Charges of the Mutual Fund 84

Shareholder Fees and Charges 85

Annual Expenses on Operations 85

Selling of Mutual Fund Shares 86

Factors to Consider in Selling Mutual Fund Shares 87

What Happens When There is a Change in the Mutual Fund 87

The Costs of A Mutual Fund 89

The Expense-Ratio 92

Chapter 6: Tips to Ensure that Your Mutual Funds are Profitable **95**

Tip 1: Be Very Careful with the Mutual Funds' Expense Ratio ... 96

Tip 2: Do Not Invest in Mutual Funds with High Turnover Ratios 97

Tip 3: Your Mutual Funds Must Have a Disciplined, Knowledgeable and Experienced Money Management Team ... 99

Tip 4: Your Mutual Funds Must Have Sufficient Asset Diversification 100

Tip 5: The Dollar Cost Average 101

Chapter 7:Retirement Income Planning on Mutual Funds **105**

Retirement Planning 107

The SIP's Method of Capacity 112

401(k) and 403(b) Plans 113

The Powers of Compounding Money..................................114

The Powers of Compounding Money II.............................115

Chapter 8: Strategies Used by Mutual Fund Managers 119

Bottom-Up or Top-Down Investing..119

Technical or Fundamental Analysis......................................121

Contrarian Investing..121

Dividend Investing...122

Chapter 9: Mutual Fund Taxation 123

Mutual Fund Regulations..125

The System Regulating Mutual Funds.................................126

The Security and Exchange Commission (SEC).....................126

Office of Compliance Inspections and Examinations...........127

Office of Investor Education and Assistance (OIEA) 128

Department of Labor..128

NASD Regulation, Inc...129

Internal Revenue Service (IRS) 129

The Fund Directors...129

Mutual Fund Data 130

Mutual Fund Performance 131

Comparison between Exchange Trade and Mutual Funds...132

Scenarios on when to Bid Goodbye to Mutual Funds 133

How to Manage Portfolios 139

Time Duration: 139

Risk 140

Amount..141

Portfolio Concentration 141

Chapter 10: Performance Measures of Mutual Fund................143

The Sharpe Measure 145

Treynor Measure.. 146

Jenson Model 146

Fama Model 147

Conclusion...149

Introduction

I want to take this moment to thank you and acknowledge you for considering the book, Mutual Funds: Comprehensive Beginner's Guide to Create Wealth using Mutual Funds.

Without any doubts, everyone yearns and desires to achieve financial freedom. Maybe you want to retire some years from now or maybe you want to start a small catering business. Perhaps you want to save money for your children's college education, or maybe you want to have a lump sum in order to pay for the new family car.

It does not matter what your specific achievements are, all things will be swift the moment you attain true financial freedom.

The question now arises: How can an individual gain financial freedom?

In real life, there are many ways to reach the final destination of being financially secure and independent.

For example, you can work your way up the corporate ladder and save some money from your salary, or you can start a small business that you know is sorely needed by the community. Of course you could always venture into the foreign exchange trading or stock market

Among the most operational and guaranteed ways of financial independence is through investing in mutual funds. This guide aims to teach you all about attaining financial independence through investing in mutual funds.

You are about to learn a variety of proven steps and strategies on how to strategically invest your money in mutual funds with the goal of achieving financial independence.

You will find that the overall goal of this book is to provide you with the basic principles of mutual funds investing so you can get started with a feeling of confidence. The aim of this guide is to provide you with advanced strategies on how to make your investments profitable so that you can readily apply them to a growing mutual fund portfolio.

You will further find the information in this guide as highly practical, and effective. As you go through each chapter, you will be able to apply what you learn in the real world immediately. Only the essential principles and dynamics of the mutual funds' industry are outlined in order to inspire you to invest!

Also, you can rest assured that unnecessary jargon that is highly technical is deliberately not included in order to be simple and easy to understand even if you have never invested before. This will make the general tone of this book as intuitive and easy to learn as possible.

Once you truly learn and understand the basic principles and strategies that need to be applied in order to make your investment in mutual funds worthwhile, financial independence will no doubt come to you soon!

The ground rules of mutual fund investing

The world of investments has several ground rules meant for investors who are novices in their own right and wish to enter the myriad world of investments. These come in handy, for there is every possibility of losing what one has if due care is not taken.

Assess yourself: Self-assessment of one's needs, expectations and risk profile are of prime importance failing which one will make more mistakes in putting money in the right places than otherwise. One should identify the degree of risk-bearing capacity one has and also clearly state the expectations from the investments. Irrational expectations will only bring pain.

Try to understand where the money is going: It is important to identify the nature of investment and to know if one is compatible with the investment. One can lose substantially if one picks the wrong kind of mutual fund. In order to avoid any confusion it is better to go through the literature, such as offer documents and fact sheets, that mutual fund companies provide on their funds.

Don't rush in picking funds, think first: One first has to decide what he wants the money for and it is this investment goal that should be the guiding light for all investments. Therefore, it is crucial to understand the risks associated with the fund and align it with the quantum risk one is willing to take. One should take a look at the portfolio of the funds for the purpose. Excessive exposure to any specific sector should be avoided, as it will only add to the risk of the entire portfolio. Mutual funds invest with a certain ideology such as the "Value Principle" or "Growth Philosophy." Both have their share of critics but both philosophies work for investors of different kinds. Identifying the proposed investment philosophy of the fund will give insight into the kind of risks that shall be taken in the future.

Invest. Don't speculate: A common investor is limited to the degree of risk that he is willing to take. It is thus of key importance that there is thought given to the process of investment and to the time horizon of the intended investment. One should abstain from speculating, which in other words would mean getting out of one fund and investing in another with the intention of making quick money. One would do well to remember that nobody can perfectly time the market so staying invested is the best option unless there are compelling reasons to exit.

Don't put all the eggs in one basket: This old-age adage is of utmost importance. No matter what the risk profile of a person is, it is always advisable to diversify the risks associated. So putting one's money in different asset classes is generally the best option as it averages the risks in each category. Thus, even investors of equity should be judicious and invest some portion of the investment in debt. Diversification even in any particular asset class (such as equity, debt) is good. Not all fund managers have the same acumen of fund management and with an identification of the best man being a tough task, it is good to place money in the hands of several fund managers. This might reduce the maximum return possible, but will also reduce the risks.

Be regular: Investing should be a habit and not an exercise undertaken at one's wishes, if one has to really benefit from them. As we said earlier, since it is extremely difficult to know when to enter or exit the market, it is important to beat the market by being systematic. The basic philosophy of Rupee cost averaging would suggest that if one regularly invests through the ups and downs of the market, he will stand a better chance of generating more returns than the market for the entire duration. The SIPs (Systematic Investment Plans) offered by all funds helps in being systematic. The one thing one should do is give post-dated cheques to the fund and one will not be harried later.

The Automatic Investment Plans offered by some funds goes a step further, as the amount can be directly/electronically transferred from the account of the investor.

Do your homework: It is important for all investors to research the avenues available to them irrespective of the investor category they belong to. This is important because an informed investor is in a better decision to make right decisions. Having identified the risks associated with the investment is important and so one should try to know all aspects associated with it. Asking intermediaries is one of the ways to take care of the problem.

Find the right funds: Finding funds that do not charge a higher fee is of importance, as the fee charged ultimately goes from the pocket of the investor. This is even more important for debt funds as the returns from these funds are not much. Funds that charge more will reduce the yield to the investor. Finding the right funds is important and one should also use these funds for tax efficiency. Investors of equity should keep in mind that all dividends are currently tax-free in India and so their tax liabilities can be reduced if the dividend payout option is used. Investors of debt will be charged a tax on dividend distribution and so can easily avoid the payout options.

Keep track of your investments: Finding the right fund is important but even more important is to keep track of the way they are performing in the market. If the market is beginning to enter a bearish phase, investors of equity too will benefit by switching to debt funds as the losses can be minimized. One can always switch back to equity if the equity market starts to show some buoyancy.

Know when to sell your mutual funds: Knowing when to exit a fund is also of utmost importance. One should book profits immediately when enough has been earned i.e. the initial expectation from the fund has been met. Other factors, like non-performance, hike in a fee charged, and change in any basic attribute of the fund, etc. are some of the reasons to exit. Investments in mutual funds, too, are not risk-free and so investments warrant some caution and careful attention of the investor. Investing in mutual funds can be a dicey business for people who do not remember to follow these rules diligently, as people are likely to commit mistakes by being ignorant or adventurous enough to take risks more than what they can absorb. This is the reason why people would do well to remember these rules before they set out to invest their hard-earned money.

Thanks again for choosing this guide.

Let's get started.

Mutual Funds

CHAPTER 1

Understanding Mutual Funds

A mutual fund is a collection of money from individual investors, businesses, and other financial groups. A mutual fund company hires a "fund manager" to grow the money contributed by the investors.

In other words also, a mutual fund is a way of investing in stock markets. A lot of investors pool their money to invest. A manager or a team of managers invest on behalf of all investors, for a fee. Every investor cannot be highly qualified for the purpose of stock investing. The main purpose of building a mutual fund is to bring in experience and expertise to the investing.

Mutual funds have been around for a very long time. In recent years, the regulations on Mutual funds have tightened, giving benefit to the investors.

That moment one purchases an MF, the cash is combined with other investor's money, and stocks of companies are bought. The investors are then allotted units of the mutual fund, whose value is the equivalent to a part of the underlying stocks. Any dividends earned on the underlying stocks are distributed among the MF unit holders.

The underlying stocks in a fund are chosen as per the investment objectives of the investors. Also, if the investors wish to invest in a specific sector, like information technology or pharmaceutical companies, then they may select a fund which specifically chooses stocks of that sector.

The most attractive feature of Mutual funds is the ease of investments. You pool up the money along with other investors and the experienced fund managers do all the hard work and research for you.

The second reason to seriously consider it is the possibility that your money is put in the stock markets. That is the obvious reason to invest in Mutual funds. The money put in stocks is no doubt risky, but also rewarding.

The Structure of Mutual Funds

A mutual fund is structured like a corporation or a business trust. This means that, like any other corporation, mutual funds are owned by the shareholders.

These funds are externally managed, so they do not have employees. Instead, mutual funds are run by affiliate organizations and independent contractors.

Here are the parties that are involved in the running and operation of a mutual fund.

The mutual fund manager: The manager is responsible for establishing the mutual fund, marketing and overseeing its general administration.

Portfolio adviser: This is the professional financial manager appointed by the Fund Manager to oversee the fund's investment options. The mutual fund manager can also act as the portfolio adviser.

Principal Distributor: This person is responsible for coordinating the sale of the funds to investors directly or through registered dealers.

Custodian: This is the bank of the trust company appointed by the Mutual Fund Manager to hold the securities owned by the fund.

Transfer agent and registrar: This person is responsible for maintaining the list of investors or shareholders in the fund.

Auditor: This is an independent auditor contracted by the mutual fund manager to conduct an annual audit and provide a report on the fund's financial statement.

Trustee: This is the entity that has the title to the fund's securities on behalf of the shareholders in cases where the funds are organized as trusts rather than corporations

Mutual fund returns are based on luck. Although companies will promise to give back your money along with a profit, this is not always the case. Once the money is put into the market, units will be allotted to the individual investors. If you wish to invest in it, then you must understand all the risks that come with it.

Classes of Mutual Funds

A mutual fund has different classes of shares. A class invests in a similar pool of securities. It has the same investment policies and goals. Furthermore, it has different services offered to shareholders as well as distribution arrangements with different expenses and fees. As such, a class has a different result in terms of performance. If a fund has a multi-class framework, it means that investors can choose the expense structure as well as fees that will meet his investment goals.

A mutual fund with Class A Shares has a front-end sales loan with minimal 12b-1 fee and yearly expenses as compared to the other classes. There are mutual funds which lower the front-end load when the investor's investment is increased. If investing in Class A Shares, it is important to ask the broker or mutual fund company representative about breakpoints. Class B Shares mutual fund has no front-end sales load but charges a 12b-1 fee as well as a contingent sales load. The shares can be automatically converted to a class with a reduced 12b-1 fee if the shares are held by the investor long enough. A mutual fund with Class C Shares charges annual expenses, a 12b-1 fee, and either a back- or front-end sales load. However, the sales load is much lower than the other classes. Class C Shares aren't convertible to other classes and have higher yearly expenses.

How Mutual Funds Work

A mutual fund is actually an organization which collects investors' money to invest them in bonds, stocks, short term money-market products, other assets or securities, or a combination of any of these products. This holdings mix is referred to as a portfolio. Every share an investor has is representative of his proportionate ownership of the income and holdings of the mutual fund.

A mutual fund, also known as an open-ended company, is a major kind of an investment company. There are also companies, which are known as closed-end funds, which offer shares through an initial public offering and these shares are then traded on a secondary market. A unit investment trust, on the other hand, offers a public offering of redeemable securities. These securities become worthless when the trust reaches its termination date. On the other hand, an exchange-traded fund, is an investment company which tries to mimic similar return like a specific market index.

Characteristics of a Mutual Fund

A mutual fund offers shares to investors directly or through a broker. It isn't transacted on any major exchanges like the NASDAQ or the New York Stock Exchange. The value of each share is determined on the fund's net asset value plus any fees collected by the fund when the investor buys shares. Each share is redeemable. It can be bought back by the fund. A mutual fund can sell shares to new investors. The mutual fund's investments are often managed by a team of experienced investment advisers who are SEC-registered.

Net Asset Value of a Mutual Fund

The mutual fund's net asset value is the market value per share of the fund. It is actually the price an investor must pay if he wants to buy shares of the fund. It is also the price the fund will pay if the investor sells his shares back to the fund. The net asset value is computed by dividing the total value of the fund, minus its liabilities, by the total number of outstanding shares. This amount is computed daily upon the close of trading. The mutual fund distributes almost all of its gains and income to its investors. As such, the net asset value mustn't be used as a measure of the performance of the fund. The fund's performance is best analyzed by its total return.

Advantages of Investing in Mutual Funds

A mutual fund is professionally managed. It has a pool of expert money managers who research, choose, and monitor the securities the fund buys. Investors can diversify their portfolios by investing in mutual funds. Instead of owning different bonds or stocks, they buy mutual funds to reduce their risks of losing money. A mutual fund investment is also more affordable than other types of investments. Furthermore, it is easy to buy and sell mutual fund shares. Investors can buy shares from a mutual fund company. They can also sell back the same shares to the company anytime.

Asset diversification is important in investing. Every investor seeks ways to mitigate risks inherent in investing by distributing his hard-earned money to different investment vehicles. Diversification may be costly to a retail investor because he has to invest in various investments to attain a diversified portfolio. If he buys shares in a mutual fund, he immediately enjoys the benefits of diversification without necessarily investing a lot of money. However, he must check first if the mutual fund invests in a particular sector or industry only. If this is the case, this fund doesn't offer diversification benefits.

Another important benefit of a mutual fund is that it offers economies of scale, which means that the cost of a thing becomes cheaper if it is bought in bulk. A mutual fund is able to take advantage of economies of scale. Transaction costs are reduced, and the investor need not pay commissions for numerous stocks he needs for diversification. By investing in a mutual fund, less money is spent on transaction fees. Furthermore, an investor can buy mutual fund shares in smaller denominations. Therefore, he can buy shares periodically to take advantage of cost averaging. He need not wait to raise enough money to invest in a mutual fund. He can buy shares on a monthly basis.

It is also easy to enter and exit a mutual fund investment. An investor can easily sell his shares back to the mutual fund company. But, he has to check if the company charges any fee for selling the shares. Lastly, buying mutual fund shares is like selecting an expert money manager. The investor buys shares because he believes that the fund's manager will be able to grow his money.

Liquidity - The people who invest their capital in mutual funds can easily get their money back. In general, they can sell their mutual funds in a short timeframe without experiencing significant reductions in the market price. However, you should consider the fees that can be applied to your transactions.

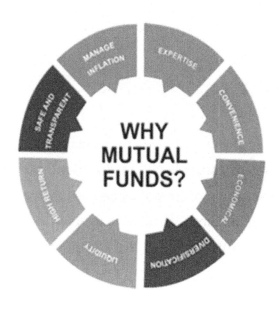

Disadvantages of Investing in Mutual Funds

The disadvantage of investing in mutual funds is that the companies charge a large amount as fees. Many of these fees are based on the fund type and the fund's risk level. If you are interested in day trading, then mutual funds would not be the right choice for you. There can arise a small delay in the mutual fund investment, and if you miss out on buying the stocks you were interested in, then your mutual fund investment will be a waste.

Mutual funds are great choices for anyone interested in investing for a long time. There is no point in making an investment today and expecting the results tomorrow. Whether it is the stock market or mutual funds, you need to wait for it to grow in value. There are mutual funds that vary in size and investment time. Three to four years is the minimum investment time for mutual funds Shorter terms are available, but these will not pay you a great return.

Mutual fund investments are of two types: open-ended and close-ended funds. Open-ended funds are those that enable investors to access their investment and receive regular returns on it. Close-ended funds, on the other hand, are fixed and will not provide investor access. They are locked in and will not offer investors with any regular income. Investors can look at their net asset value at the end of the day, and that's about it. However, when the mutual fund reaches maturity, the investors can get all the benefits at once.

Another problem is inflation. If you want to avoid inflation problems, it is better to avoid mutual funds and stick to stocks, as stocks have the ability to fluctuate. It is great to remember that like all investments, mutual funds are unpredictable, as inflation can lessen the value of the bond.

Another disadvantage of a mutual fund is that the investor has to pay fees annually, even if the fund doesn't perform well. Furthermore, taxes may be levied on the distribution of capital gains. The investor also has no control of the fund's portfolio. He can't influence the fund manager to buy and sell securities he wants. Furthermore, the net asset value is computed at the end of trading. The investor has no idea how much the NAV is during the day. Therefore, he doesn't know if he will buy or sell his mutual fund shares until after the NAV gets computed.

Like other investment products, a mutual fund doesn't guarantee a return on investment because it is always possible for the fund's value to depreciate. Its price can fluctuate if the securities fluctuate. Therefore, an investor who wants to invest in a mutual fund must do research first. A mutual fund is also not guaranteed by the government. Therefore, the investor may not get back his investment if the mutual fund company is dissolved. Most investors in mutual funds over-diversify their portfolio. They often acquire various mutual funds from different providers.

Therefore, they don't benefit from diversification because they're overdoing it. On the other hand, investing in one mutual fund doesn't mean that the investor has diversified his portfolio because there are mutual funds which are invested in one industry or sector only.

A mutual fund company needs to have a lot of stand-by cash in cases when investors sell back their shares to the company. Although it keeps the company liquid, too much idle cash has its disadvantage as well. Also, investing in mutual funds can be costly. Mutual fund companies employ experienced money managers so that these firms can boast of excellent professional management. However, the overall payout is reduced because the investor has to pay various fees like annual operating fees and shareholder fees. The investor pays shareholder fees when he buys or sells mutual fund shares. He is charged as much as 3% for annual operating fees. He has to pay these fees even if the fund didn't perform well.

Some mutual fund companies engage in misleading advertisements in order to entice investors to sign up with them. Some funds advertise themselves incorrectly as growth funds, income funds, or small-cap funds. In order for a mutual fund to be called as a particular type of fund, the Securities and Exchange Commission requires a specific mutual fund to have a minimum of 80% of its assets in a specific kind of investment.

Other companies use other names to make it attractive and misleading.

Lastly, investors find it difficult to research and evaluate the different mutual funds because mutual fund investing doesn't offer tools to compare different companies. The NAV of a mutual fund company cannot be compared to the NAV of another company. Ratings, ranking, and advertisements only describe the previous performances of the company. This information has no value because as good performance in the past isn't a guarantee that it will perform better now and in the future.

How to set and manage your investment goals

All this information can be daunting, but do not fear. We will take it to step by step, starting from the top. Unsure where to start? Start with your own profile, and think about what you and your family need. With a pen and notebook, jot down your investment goals. The first things you need to identify are what you are saving for and when you need the money. Then, we review below some metrics you can use to pick the right mutual fund to suit your risk profile and investment goals.

How in-depth you need to go roughly correlates to how long you will be holding the investment instrument before selling it. Casual investors, investing for years or decades in anticipation of college tuitions or retirement, will be well-prepared if they carefully understand the following details of the mutual fund:

Long-term performance information:

How has the fund performed over the past 5, 10, or 20 years? The prospectus has valuable insight into performance in its risk/return bar chart and table, which shows you the fund's pre- and post-tax annual total returns over the last ten years. The same values are given for a composite benchmark index to provide you with some standard of comparison. However, to really understand the fund's objectives and performance, you need a point of comparison. Look online to compare the fund's performance with its "peer group", these are other funds which have similar objectives and strategies. It is a good sign if your pick performs well against both the benchmark index and members of its peer group.

Fees:

Since all mutual funds are registered with the SEC, they have to comply with the requirement to publish a fee table in their prospectus. This breaks down all the fees you may be subject to. Paying fees is not desirable as it eats into your returns, but these allow the mutual fund company, ultimately a profit-seeking business, to cover its costs. Fees are detailed below.

Expense ratios:

At the bottom of the prospectus' fee table will be the expense ratio, which sums all the fund's annual operating expenses as a fraction of its average net assets. This is useful to compare across funds. The moment you have analyzed your options, it is highly advisable to use a mutual fund cost calculator (you can find one on the SEC's official website) to compare your options.

Risk:

To analyze the risk of investing in a particular mutual fund, keep your eye on two factors: the beta, which measures the fund's volatility against the S&P 500, and the fund's biggest quarterly loss, which shows you how bad things can get if you invest with them.

It is sensible to spend some more time on fees and expenses as they differentiate mutual funds from most other investments. They go towards paying the professional money manager who increases your returns, but they also eat away at those same returns over time.

A load is a cost of buying or selling shares of a mutual fund. It is the sales charge, and the most common fee in a mutual fund. Loaded mutual funds can sometimes charge 5% or more, and these fees go to the fund company and the broker. Generally, avoid loads. They are unnecessary losses. So why do they exist? Investment gurus might posit that loads lock you into a particular investment for a longer time—just like if you pay a $20 cover charge to get into a new bar, you are likely to stay there longer than if you'd entered for free. This can be a win-win situation because it keeps you invested beyond short-term fluctuations in the market, and the fund has more capital to work with. You are less likely to sell and pay another load for another investment. But paying a load is not in your best interest, and even avoiding loaded mutual funds will leave you with a whole lot of great options to choose from.

You need to be cautious when reading the prospectus with regards to fees. Keep in mind that, up until 0.25% per year, a fund can be labeled a no-load fund. Still, there may be other fees. For example, a 12b-1 fee is something some mutual funds charge for their "distribution or service," essentially implying a fee to cover their marketing expenses. These fees should generally be avoided. Funds can charge several other fees, such as redemption fees (sales charge paid to the fund rather than the broker), account fees (charged for maintaining accounts, often when they are below a certain value), exchange fees, and purchase fees (similar to a load).

A note about using past performance to estimate your returns: it is not a done deal. Previous performance does not determine future performance, and this is because managers are constantly changing the underlying securities and the stock market is inherently unpredictable. When you can, and you should, use indicators of past performance to get an idea of how volatile the fund is. If this is too risky for your taste, look elsewhere. How do you know how much risk you can take? Remember that volatility is smoothed over time with the general upward trend of the market, so short-term investments are riskier. For example, if you are investing your retirement money, you might be fine with volatile investments since you are investing for the long-term. However, if there is a chance that you could need that money sooner, and you may use it as an emergency fund five years from now, you will find risk less acceptable than someone investing it for 20 years. Risk not only depends on your financial goals but also your personal preference. If you know you would rather not see your returns swing up and down, even if it results in high returns, stick with low-risk (and low-return) investments.

Remember, the money market is less risky than bonds, which in turn is less risky than stocks. So if you are saving for the short term, look to money market funds. Investing long term? You can feel comfortable with the volatility of stocks. Somewhere in the middle? Bonds are good for financial goals that are five to ten years into the future, and you can balance your portfolio with money market and stock investments.

With mutual funds, you must pay an income tax on any dividends you receive from the fund in a particular year. When you sell your shares, your personal capital gains will be taxed. In addition, as a member of the mutual fund, you will be also be taxed on the fund's capital gains. If a fund collects income through dividends or by selling securities for a profit, shareholders have to chip in to pay those taxes. This means you may be paying taxes even though you didn't personally collect capital gains from the fund. Steer clear of big tax hits by investing in tax-efficient funds and tax-exempt funds.

Safety of money in mutual funds:

When we talk about the safety of money in any investment vehicle, we are talking about the probability of frauds and the certainty of returns.

For example, when you invest in a savings account, you are investing your money with a well-known bank, so you are certain that your money is safe from any frauds. At the same time, you get a commitment from the bank that you will get a certain interest rate. Hence, you are certain about your return on investment.

Mutual funds are not as safe as the savings or fixed deposit accounts with your bank, but they offer a probability of higher returns than these safer investments. No mutual fund guarantees the rate of return.

Usually, the funds are set up under the umbrella of a reputed financial institution, mostly banks. For some investors, this is enough assurance that their money is not prone to fraud.

The return on investments in a mutual fund is highly uncertain. They are linked with the performance of stock markets. Looking back at the history of stock markets, you can see that they are very volatile, though, with some smart management of stocks, you may end up making decent returns.

The picking and timely selling of stocks is best left to the qualified professionals. The mutual funds, though risky as discussed above, offer a probability of good returns, and hence are offer a good risk-reward ratio.

Mutual Funds

CHAPTER 2

Types of Mutual Funds

There are distinguished types of mutual funds – bond funds, money market funds, stock funds, and many more as discussed below. Each of these types of mutual funds has a specific amount of risk and return involved. Before choosing one of them, determine your financial goals and your risk temperament first. As a universal rule, the more the potential return, the higher the risk of loss.

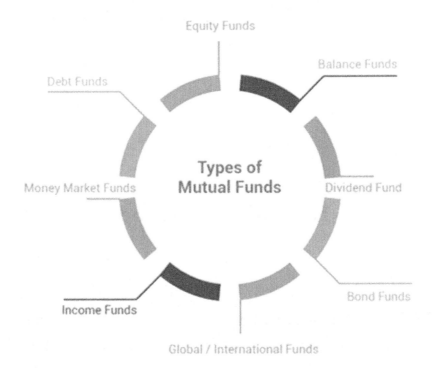

Mutual Funds Based on Bonds

Bond funds include treasury bonds, insured bonds, and other types of bonds usually bought in the bond market. Generally, bond funds have higher risk and return ratios as compared to money market funds. However, bond funds have lower risk and return ratios when compared to stock funds. The major risks that are involved when it comes to bond funds are the following:

- Risk of the interest rate

- Risk on the credit

- Risk of prepayment

With respect to the risk of the interest rate: Remember that when the interest rates go down, the market value of the bonds will rise. Conversely, as the interest rates go up, the market value of the bonds will diminish. As such, should the interest rates go up after your investment, you can lose serious money.

With respect to the risk on credit: Remember that there are basically two types of bonds:

Bonds that are lower risk such as insured bonds and treasury bonds; and

The ones that are at higher risk are such as bonds issued by individual companies.

Basically, if the bonds fund you chose is composed of lower risk bonds (the first type), you will have lower risks on credit. The reason is that a state (i.e., USA, UK, Russia, Japan, China) is always liquid and will be able to pay its debts without resorting to legal remedies. A state can never be bankrupt. The downside however, is that lower risk bonds provide lower returns for investors.

However, if the bonds fund you chose is composed of higher risk bonds (the second type), you will have higher risks on credit. This is because corporations, partnerships and other kinds of businesses use various forms of leverage in order to grow. Due to such, there will always exist a risk that they will not be able to pay their credit on time. Should this happen, they will go bankrupt. The upside however, is that higher risk bonds provide higher returns for investors.

With respect to the risk on the prepayment: This refers to the risk that the bond might be paid off earlier than the due date. As an illustrative example, suppose that after you invest in a bonds fund, the interest rates fall. The implication of this is that the market value of the bonds which comprise your mutual fund portfolio will increase. This is a downside because the issuer of the bond will opt to pay the debt earlier than due and issue another set of bonds that have lower rates. Should this happen, the mutual fund will not be able to reinvest the profits in another set of bonds that may pay a higher rate. Instead, the mutual fund company will be forced to buy the set of bonds issued by the bond issuer that have lower rates of return.

Mutual Funds Based on Money Market Assets or Securities

Money market funds are mutual funds that are composed of money market assets and securities. Compared to other types of mutual funds, money market funds are relatively low risk. Conversely, the potential returns are also considerably low. If you are living in the United States, the rules when it comes to money market funds are as follows, according to the Securities and Exchange Commission:

Money market funds can only invest in short term investments;

Money market funds can only invest in high-quality securities or assets;

Money market funds can only invest in securities or assets that are duly issued by any of the following:

- The USA Federal Government

- USA state and local governments

- A duly licensed USA Corporation

More often than not, the returns (or profit) of a money market fund will generally reflect the interest rates in the short term. In addition, the returns of a money market fund are generally lower than that of bond and stock funds.

The major risk of investing in a money market fund is the risk of inflation. This means that the rate of inflation might outpace the returns of a money market fund.

Mutual Funds Based on Equities or Stocks

Stock funds are mutual funds that are basically composed of equities or stocks. Equities or stocks refer to the proportion of one's ownership in a publicly listed corporation in terms of shares. Publicly listed corporations are those corporations that can be bought by the public in stock exchanges such as the NASDAQ and the New York Stock Exchange. This means that the stock fund will pick a set of stock from a given stock exchange.

Mutual funds based on stocks are characterized by high levels of volatility, similar to that of equities in the stock market. This means that the value of the mutual fund can rise and fall quickly over a short period of time. However, research in wealth and finance have already found that investments in equities have historically performed better than any other type of asset.

However, not all stock funds are alike. There are also different types of stock funds in order to meet the specific needs, financial goals and risk the desire of different investors. Listed below are the 4 basic types of stock funds:

- Income stock funds

- Growth stock funds

- Sector stock funds

- Stock Market Index funds

Income stock funds are mutual funds that invest in equities that pay regular amounts of dividends every year or every quarter to its shareholders.

Growth stock funds are mutual funds that invest in equities that are found to have lots of growth potential. As such, investors would like to profit from these kinds of mutual funds through capital gains or capital appreciation.

Sector stock funds are mutual funds that invest in equities from a specific industry segment. For example, there are sector stock funds that solely invest in consumer products such as Kraft and McDonald's. Also, there are sector stock funds that solely invest in technology such as Apple and Microsoft.

Stock Market Index funds are mutual funds that invest in equities that are listed in a specific stock market index (in whole or in part). The goal of this type of stock fund is to have a return or profits that are similar to the specific stock market index chosen.

Income Funds

Another type of mutual funds is quite popular and is known as income funds. As the name suggests, they are used to derive a regular income and are thus employed as an investment scheme to end up with a fixed income on a monthly basis. A mutual fund never sticks to any one kind of investment and helps in diversifying your risk. So when it comes to income funds, the mutual fund scheme will not limit itself to just one kind of investment. It will look for several inner compositions for all its varieties. Thus, income funds will also be split up, and the fund manager will invest a person's money in all of its varieties. These varieties are given below.

A real estate investment trust is one in which the shareholders are paid a regular income for the real estate investments they make. This means that the shareholder is contributing towards the building and upkeep of real estate ventures, such as shopping malls, metros, office spaces, etc. Whatever the trust earns is split up and distributed to the shareholders. These shareholders will, therefore, derive a fixed sum of money from such investments.

Master limited partnerships. Master limited partnerships are those holdings where the company diversifies into separate subsidiaries. It will then allow the shareholder units that will comprise all the different subsidiaries. The shareholder will get paid whatever is earned by the different subsidiaries on a monthly basis.

Royalty Trusts. Royalty trusts, such as the U.S. royalty trust, pay their shareholders money on a regular basis. These trusts will hold enterprises, such as oil and gas. However, this type has seen a sharp decline in the past few years, and mutual fund managers refrain from investing their shareholders' money in such trusts. Government bond investments are seen as being safer options than private investments. This is mainly because they are sure of not going bad, and even if they do, the government will ensure that all the shareholders receive their money.

The main advantage is the dividends that investors receive. However, there are disadvantages as well. It takes longer to see any returns, as the profits from the investment are used to give dividends but not investment growth. Another important risk is the chance of interruptions, which means that the issuer, for whatever reason, cannot make dividends. It's important to see if this fund is worth the risk for you.

Balanced Funds

A balanced fund is a hybrid mutual fund. It combines three to four different elements of financial securities. It takes a few stocks, some bond or income funds, as well as a few market investments and then prepares a combined portfolio. The idea of a balanced fund is to help investors diversify both their risk and income gain. Thus, by having a balanced fund, investors can have a regular income and remain invested for a long time. Balanced funds are great options for beginners looking to increase their financial holdings and diversifying their investments, as these funds are very simple. They are very easy to understand, as this type of fund is just balancing the risks and rewards of investing.

The general rule is to have 60% as your fixed investment and 40% as your regular income investment. The choice is yours, and you can select a combination that works for you, but remember that there will be a minimum investment clause, and you will have to invest whatever is expected of you.

There is the option of changing up the portfolio mix from time to time. This means that it is not necessary to hold on to the same kind of investment for long. If you feel like a particular aspect of your balanced fund mix is not working for you, then you can change it to something else that works in your favor. This kind of freedom is not available for other forms of mutual fund investments. Your fund manager will keep you updated on your incomes and also let you choose whether you stay or take an exit on the fund. In most cases, the manager himself will take a call on whether to exit a fund or not. He will keep switching it up depending on market conditions and how the economy is moving.

Like all investments, it has disadvantages, such as the management fee being the same no matter how the market is performing. Moreover, it is not recommended to those who are in a lower tax bracket, as returns are very moderate, so to see a large return, you will need to invest a lot of money.

Equity Funds

Equity funds are another type of investment that the mutual fund encompasses. Here, there are three distinct qualities that the mutual fund manager looks at, namely, growth, value, and a mixture of the two. When you invest in an equity fund, you are looking at the growth of the company that you are investing in and their holding. This refers to how significantly the investment will grow over the course of time and what dividends the company will pay once it achieves a higher profit. Value refers to how valuable it will get over time or if it already is a big company. So you are looking for these both individually and as a combined output.

There are large cap options, mid-cap options, and small-cap options. It is entirely up to you to decide where you want to invest. Say, for example, you choose a well-established company that has a large business but does not have a good share price; this will be considered a large value investment. Conversely, say you invest in a company that has only limited finances hoping for a startup, but its share price is doing well in the market; you would call it a small growth investment.

The idea is to have some combined investments. All of them will add up to give you a combined profit in the end. The fund manager will suggest the best options that you can consider for your investment, as he or she will have a proper idea of what investments will pay off and how. However, as the ultimate investor, it is important for you to make a choice for yourself and not solely rely on the manager's suggestions. After you have done your investigation and understood which stocks will do well, then you can suggest these to the manager and listen to his or her advice.

A great advantage of equity funds is that these funds have a great liquid value in the secondary market, so if you sell these funds, you can make a great profit. Another advantage is that managers do not charge large commission fees. It is important to check whether or not your manager will charge you a large fee for their services.

ELSS:

It is a diversified equity mutual fund. In this scheme of mutual funds, the investor gets tax benefit under 80C up to 1.5 lakh. In this fund, there is a three-year lock-in period which is lower than any other scheme which comes under 80C tax deduction. An investor also gets a higher return in this scheme than any other schemes, which comes under 80C tax deduction facilities. Moreover, the return of the fund is also not taxable whereas other schemes (NSC, Senior citizen FD) returns are. An investor can invest in ELSS under two schemes, growth and dividend.

Benefits of ELSS:

i. Market-linked –Comparatively high return

ii. Tax deduction facilities under 80C.

Common mistakes while purchasing ELSS:

i. Late investment in a financial year and lump–sum investment – As this scheme comes under 80C, investors invest in this scheme during the last period of a financial year and, as they invest late, they invest in a lump-sum. This is a mistake because they don't get the advantage of averaging and the investor gets affected by improper market timing.

ii. Too many funds– Leads to a complicated portfolio which is difficult to handle.

iii. Redeem after 3 years – As there is a lock-in period of 3 years, some investors redeem just after 3 years. It is advisable to be invested at least for 5 years or more to get a healthy return.

iv. Choosing dividend options–choosing dividend options during investment in ELSS is a blunder because, by doing so, you just might miss the power of compounding.

v. Understanding the nature of the portfolio–During the investment, you should understand the nature of the portfolio of the fund. Some funds are large-cap and others may be a mid-cap or small-cap. Returns of large-cap is steady, and risk is low. In the case of mid-cap and small-cap returns fluctuates; may be higher or lower. So during fund selection, one should select funds very carefully according to his needs and goals.

vi. Choosing fund on a short term performance basis–Choosing a fund depending on the performance of the last few months is a very big mistake because that fund may not bring a very good return in the long run. During mutual fund investments, one should always focus on a long term basis, especially for a period of 5 to 7 years.

Global Funds

Global or international funds are a unique type of mutual fund investments.

An international fund is one where the investment is compulsorily made in a country that is outside your home country. A global fund, on the other hand, is made anywhere in the world and might also include your home country. Overall, these are funds that are not limited to your state or region alone. Thus, confusing the two would be a mistake, and international funds can be considered as being bigger than global funds.

For example, a foreign currency investment is not necessarily a global fund. Foreign currency implies that you are investing in a currency that is not your own, but it is possible to invest in your own currency in certain situations. Let's say that a Texas-based investor invests in Japanese currency, and only Japanese currency. That means that the Texan is investing in a foreign fund that would be considered an international fund instead of a global one because the investor is only investing in one foreign currency, not including his or her own, which is the U.S. dollar.

The key to having this type of fund is diversification. You know how important it is for your funds to be diversified in the stock market. If you invest in global or international funds, you have the chance to invest in a unique fund that will give you good returns. You will tap not only into the potential of your own market, but also into the market of countries that might be financially stronger than yours. Now imagine having the chance to convert all your local currency into that of a country with a currency that is trailing. You will obviously come into a bigger profit.

These types of funds are popular but undoubtedly quite risky, owing to a lack of proper knowledge and inefficiency in predicting global markets. It is quite tough to tame your local market, and it will be that much tougher to tame foreign markets. Your fund manager will have to conduct a lot of research in order to nest your money in this type of fund. The returns, however, will be well worth the effort, and you might end up making double or triple whatever you are already making in your local markets.

Specialty Funds

A specialty fund is a type of mutual fund that does not adhere to the common description of mutual funds. This means that they are quite unique and concentrate on a few sectors of the market. They can be classified as follows:

Sector funds. As the name suggests, pertain to those funds that are invested in certain specific sectors alone. These can include the technology sector, the financial sector, the health sector, fast-moving consumer goods, etc. All these sectors are separated, and the fund manager will decide to invest in the one that the fund manager thinks will throw up a lucrative output. The manager will not consult the client in general, as he or she will have access to the best information in the business. It is also advisable not to waste time communicating with the clients, as the markets are extremely volatile and every second counts.

Region-specific funds. As the name suggests, region-specific funds look at investments in a particular region of the world, be it local or foreign. The idea is to incorporate a foreign investment into the portfolio. This is achievable only if the person is eligible for foreign investment. The manager will have to do some amount of research and understand the markets thoroughly. There is a certain amount of risk associated with these types of funds, and the investor should be made fully aware of these before the investment goes through. The most risk to undertake will arise if the foreign country goes into recession.

Social responsibility funds. These are funds where the manager will avoid investing in companies that indulge in illegal businesses. These can include arms and ammunition building, import and export of banned substances, etc. If these companies get into trouble, then the investor's money will be in trouble. Moreover, it is the responsibility of the investor not to promote such trade for the betterment of society.

A huge disadvantage of this fund is the fact that there is a risk of lack of portfolio diversity because you are investing in a specialized fund. While you can invest in different specialized markets, it does not mean you have a greater chance of making a profit whether you invest in one specialized market or two.

Mutual Insurance

A mutual insurance company, sometimes known as a mutual insurance fund, is an insurance company that is mainly owned by policyholders.

The advantage of this fund is the fact that it exists to make sure that the benefits promised to the policyholders are there for the long term. This means that policyholders can make decisions that will benefit them in the long run. The main disadvantage is that members are charged a premium so the company can make a profit.

This premium is like an investment because policyholders have an option of receiving either a dividend or lower premiums. This is an advantage and is the best part of paying premiums.

While mutual insurance is not similar to either of the funds in this section, it is important to mention it so as to separate it from insurance shares. Interestingly enough, mutual insurance can become publicly traded if expenses have risen. In such a situation, all the policyholders will become shareholders.

An example of a mutual insurance company is Liberty Mutual Insurance, which is policyholder owned and covers many different insurance needs, such as home, life, and car insurance.

It differs from the likes of MetLife, Aflac, and Progressive, which only focus on one or two aspects of insurance needs.

While this kind of fund might seem different from the others in this section, it is similar enough to seem important so that people will not confuse it with insurance shares.

Index Funds

Index funds, as the name suggests, refer to those funds that mimic the market indexes. Thus, if I were to formulate a portfolio, it would involve the various elements of the market index. It would be similar to condensing the market into my portfolio. Index funds are said to be independent and do not really fall under the category of mutual funds. However, for ease of understanding and practical application, they are added under mutual funds.

The main idea is to flow with the market and match its footsteps. This can be a difficult task if people do not understand how to interpret the market. The fund manager will assist in the process and explain the various elements that make up the market. The investor can then choose the different elements that comprise the portfolio.

The management fees that these types of investments require are much lower than those required by regular mutual funds, so they are a good option for all those looking to come into a good profit without having to shell out a lot of money towards mutual fund fees. The reason why these fees are lower is that managers are not as active with index funds as they are with other types of investment funds. Studies have shown that this type of fund beats actively managed funds over time.

Despite some of the advantages of index funds, there are some disadvantages. These disadvantages include a lack of flexibility because these funds are dependent on the stock market. Moreover, index funds, at best, only give average returns because there is no opportunity to outperform the market, as market indexes are based on an average of certain factors of the markets.

These form the various types of mutual funds that exist in the market, and you can choose one depending on your investment plan and how much money you have at your disposal.

Factors to consider up when setting up an investment plan

There are several factors you should put into consideration to achieve a profitable investment.

Have a plan and achievements expected

Successful investing in mutual funds begins with determining your financial goals, both short and long terms. You may have short term goals, like getting a down payment for your first home, paying for your wedding or creating an emergency fund.

On the other hand, you may have long-term goals, like paying for your college education or saving for retirement. Whatever you are saving for, setting goals will help you asses the amount of money you will need to invest, what you will earn from your investment, and when you will redeem your shares.

Your next step should involve making a realistic investment plan that will help you achieve these goals. Setting a realistic expectation about your investment based on the market performance is an important part of an investment plan that you must never overlook.

Most securities do not rise in value often; however, when they drop, the downturn can be lengthy at times. As such, having a well thought out and diversified investment plan can help you stay afloat during such downturns by giving you some measure of comfort during times of market volatility.

In addition, ensure that your plan paints a broader picture of your personal financial situation both now and where you want it to be in the future. Alongside your goals, the plan should reflect your time horizon, personal feelings about risk, and financial situation. You are better off setting your goals and creating your investment plan as soon as you can.

Remember, the sooner you set your goals and begin investing, the sooner you can put compound interest to work.

Goals vs. Time Horizon:

Generally, your goals will determine how much time you will have to invest your money. For instance, if you are 30 and investing for retirement at 65, then you will have a time horizon of 35 years before you can begin withdrawing your investment money.

Setting a time horizon is crucial because it will dictate how you invest your money. Ideally, shorter periods are ideal for conservative investments while long periods allow you to handle more risk.

Risk involved:

As already mentioned, all mutual funds come with some level of risk, including the possibility of losing your principal. As such, making an informed decision to overlook some risks can also create an opportunity for greater potential reward.

This fundamental principle of investing is referred to as the "risk/reward trade-off." When drafting your investment plan, be sure to examine your attitude towards the risks that come with investment.

Find out if stability is more important to you than higher returns or if you can tolerate short term losses for potential gains in the long term. Remember, an investment that increases in value over a short period can also plummet in value quite rapidly. However, if you have taken into account the risk/reward tradeoff, then you will understand investment volatility as an important feature for a successful long-term investment plan.

Market Timing:

Buy low, sell high may sound like great advice; however, even the savviest investor often finds it impossible to identify the exact market lows and high with precision. That is why it is wise to set aside a fixed amount into a bond or stock fund on a regular basis rather than attempting to "time the market."

How to manage your investment

Once you have decided on a mutual fund, pause and congratulate yourself! Making the transaction is relatively simple compared to all the pre-purchase research. You can purchase straight from the mutual fund, although people generally go through banks or brokers, either by making a phone call or doing it online. In addition to the current NAV per share, keep in mind that you will be charged any front-end load and other fees as detailed in the prospectus. Note that you do not purchase mutual funds from a secondary market such as the New York Stock Exchange or the NASDAQ Stock Market.

Tracking

What is there to do next after purchasing shares? Investing is a funny thing. It requires patience, leaving your investments alone to let them grow beyond short-term market fluctuations. But it also requires careful monitoring because you have to know if it is performing as expected. After all, even if your fund had performed well in the past, there is no guarantee that it will continue to perform well. You must track its performance. You can do this online or by the monthly or quarterly shareholder statement you are required to receive from the mutual fund firm. It is important to safely store these statements for accounting purposes as well as tracking. Track all the metrics that you used to make your selection, and make sure they do not stray far from your expectations.

Divesting

Successful mutual fund investors always know from the onset how long they want to keep their money in a certain fund. Generally, financial experts do not suggest pulling out investments when the market is not doing so well. In the case of mutual funds, there are some circumstances under which you might consider divesting sooner than you originally intended. Reasons to divest include the following:

- Based on a regular overview of the quarterly statements, you may find that the portfolio has been rebalanced in a way that increases risk or that moves away from achieving the objectives stated in the prospectus. This is known as "style drift." This can be dangerous and should cause you to consider transferring the investment.

- Another common reason for diverting from a mutual fund is a change in managers. Often managers are careful to stick to a certain recognizable style, but, as can happen with a change in leadership, a new manager can rock the boat in ways that the shareholders do not appreciate.

- The expense ratio may rise, making it too large to be worth your while.

Remember that these performance-related issues will be reflected in the prospectus and online data—your mutual fund will decrease in rank relative to the benchmark, or the listed expense ratio will rise relative to its peer groups.

There are personal reasons to divest as well. You may be moving closer to retirement and want to shift to financial investments with generally higher returns, like stocks. You may have grown more comfortable with researching about financial opportunities and have found something better! These are all possible and valid reasons to pull out of your investment. However, always consider the pros and cons of divesting very carefully before making a decision.

You pull out of a mutual fund quite like how you would pull out of stock: make a phone call to whoever executed the trade for you. Or if you have online access, sell your shares. Selling shares are akin to taking your money out of their fund. You will have to specify how you want to receive your profits, either as a check, bank transfer, or as credit in your brokerage account so you may reinvest it, usually without paying another sales load.

CHAPTER 3

Top Mistakes to Avoid
When Venturing in Mutual Funds

All right, you now know the breakdown of the mutual fund system, you know how to choose the right manager for you, and you know how to evaluate and keep an eye on your options when it comes to the different kinds of funds you can choose.

The pros and cons will always be there in any system, and many things you learn by experience before you can know for certain what choice to make.

But there are still common mistakes many first-time investors make, and I want to help you avoid doing them yourself. Indeed, this list is not all-inclusive, and you will have to be careful not to make any mistakes as you begin, but here's a good place to start.

Avoid going for the wrong managers.

Just because a manager did well last year, doesn't mean that's going to happen again. When it comes to choosing the professional manager for your stock and your money, start your researching skills now.

Reviews and other experiences are important to take into consideration when it comes to choosing your manager, but you do have to realize that when it comes down to it, it's how you handle the stocks that matter. Look into the real business aspect of the firm before you hire.

Choosing the Right Fund Manager

The most important step in any investment decision is the research. It is the most time-consuming and resource-intensive, but also the most important step in ensuring great profits. After all, once you have chosen an investment, all you have left to do is invest the money and watch it pay you returns.

You may have heard of Vanguard and Fidelity Investments. Though these are popular mutual funds and may be good choices for your investment, it is advisable to look a little deeper before putting your money in any investment. After all, there are over 8,000 publicly traded mutual funds in the United States. How can you tell which is the best pick for you specifically? The following guidelines will help out.

The prospectus

A prospectus is a document provided by the mutual fund company to anyone who is interested in buying shares of the fund. It includes valuable information like the fund's past performance, fees and expenses, major risks in investing in mutual funds, investment strategies employed by the fund company, and the fund's investment goals. It also includes a list of the fund's advisers and managers. It also shares information on how to buy and sell the mutual fund shares. The Securities and Exchange Commission requires a mutual fund to print pertinent information in the prospectus as well as include important current data like past performance and fees in a format which can be easily understood by every investor.

Important Information in The Prospectus

The prospectus must have a date of issue printed on the front cover because investors must be provided with up-to-date information at all times. A mutual fund company must have an updated prospectus yearly. The Risk and Return Table and Bar Chart must be printed anywhere near the front pages of the prospectus. They must be found right after the description of risks, strategies, and investment objectives of the mutual fund. The bar chart must show the total annual return of the fund for the past ten years. The table of returns must show figures in before-tax and after-tax for a number of years. It must include explanations or footnotes so that investors can fully understand the information in it.

The table of fees is another important part of the fund prospectus. It usually follows the annual returns table as well as the performance bar chart. It shows both the yearly operating expenses of the fund and the shareholder fees. This table will help new investors compare different mutual funds in terms of costs. Also, the prospectus must include the financial highlights of the fund. This part is often printed at the end of the prospectus and includes audited data with regards to the annual financial performance of the fund for the past five years. It includes information about net asset values, total returns, as well as different ratios like portfolio turnover rate, net income to average net assets ratio, and expenditures to average net assets ratio.

A mutual fund profile must also be provided. It includes a summary of important information in the prospectus like investment requirements, information about the investment adviser, after-tax returns, fees and expenses, performance, major risks, major investment strategies, and investment objectives.

The Statement of Additional Information, on the other hand, discusses the operations of the mutual fund in detail. It includes the financial statement, fund history, fund policies, information about the directors and officers, tax matters, broker commissions, and performance yield as well as yearly average return on investment. This information may not be included in the prospectus but the investor can ask for a copy from the mutual fund company. An investor must be provided with a shareholder report within 2 months after the fiscal year and 2 months after the fiscal midyear. The report must include updated information about the financial status of the company. It must also include the fund's portfolio.

How to Have A Copy Of The Fund Documents

The investor can have a copy of the documents by writing or calling the mutual fund company. He can also check out its website or ask from his broker who sold him the shares. The Securities and Exchange Commission also has an Electronic Data Gathering, Analysis, and Retrieval (EDGAR) database which can be made available to the investor in order for him to download the documents at no cost.

Evaluative reports

Fund reports by investment research firms such as Morningstar and the Mutual Fund Education Alliance will help you find the right mutual funds to fit your needs. You can refer to Morningstar's Analyst Picks for investing tips and expert analysis. However, there are a plethora of other online tools that can help you compare mutual funds. If you already use certain websites like MSN Money or Yahoo! Finance for other financial matters, use them to find information on mutual funds as well.

Use a mutual fund cost calculator on the SEC website (sec.gov) to compare the costs of owning different funds before you buy.

You spend too much time and money on watching the market.

Watching the market is important. It can get expensive, especially if you never get anything to give you money back.

Do your research, yes, but also make a point of getting started as soon as you can.

You neglect to do the finer research when you have finally chosen a fund.

A fund might look bright and shiny on the outside, but, as I said in the last chapter, you have to know the little details of the fund before you know for sure that it's what you want to go with.

If the fund matches up with your goals, go for it, but make sure you do the research before you dive in.

You find a fund that's limited in what it can do.

When it comes to choosing a fund, you have to make sure you know what you are getting in to, and what your fund can do. Devote the right amount of time into the fund up front, so there are no surprises along the way.

Of course, this isn't to say that there aren't going to be risks still. There will always be risks. But you want to know what your fund can do long term, something that a good manager will be able to tell you.

You fail to understand the risks that the fund holds.

Look at the fund from all sides and be aware of what it can do and what to expect.

You overpay on things you shouldn't.

Of course, you are going to have to pay for the fees for the manager, and you will have to pay for the charges when it comes to the funds itself, but don't let yourself get nickel and dimed to death.

There are a reasonable amount of fees and charges you will pay, but do your research before you purchase to ensure you aren't getting overcharged for what you are doing.

You put too much money down up-front.

Optimism is one thing, but throwing money down on a fund when you don't have it or when you aren't sure what the facts of the stock are is quite another. Again, the fund is going to cost what it costs, but at the same time, you do have to be smart.

Put down a reasonable amount, and make sure you have the money to cover it in case you end up losing the stock. Be smart about it and think your actions through.

In other words, don't be impulsive.

You forget about taxes.

Yes, that time of year that comes up every January, you're going to have to report the money you invest and pay off the profits. Not many people realize this when they start investing, and it can get them in a lot of trouble down the road.

Make sure you do your research, even when it comes to the tax aspect, so you are well prepared to handle Uncle Sam when he comes knocking.

You scatter.

It's better to focus on one or two funds instead of trying out a whole bunch at once time. You might have the time to go through and research a variety of funds, but even if you do, it's still better to pick one or two that you enjoy and go with those.

Let them sit for a few months, and see what happens. Of course, you can add to this as you gain experience, but there's no shame in taking it easy and letting things grow. You never know where the few funds you have now are going to head.

You go too much, too soon.

As with any new thing in life, start small. There's nothing wrong with taking your time and growing what you can. If you invest all of your money in the stock market right up front, you are taking a lot of unnecessary risks.

As an alternative, add a little at a time and let it grow. . . the more you handle, the more experienced you will have, and the better you will be able to make decisions in the future. As exciting as it is, you don't have to do it all at once.

Use these mistakes as warnings of what you shouldn't do, but don't let them scare you off from mutual funds.

Now, don't let this list make you that all funds are bad, or that you are doomed to make a mistake, because you aren't. No, the intent of this list is to show you that there are a lot of things you have to keep in mind, and things you have to pay attention to, even when it comes to mutual funds.

Bear in mind that just because everyone is doing something, it doesn't imply that it's a good idea, and just because a fund has a lot of investors, or just because a management firm handled a lot of funds the previous season, it doesn't mean that it's the best choice now.

When it comes to investing, you have to look at the big picture, but nothing is as important as the present. Yes, the past can indicate what's going to happen, but in reality the past pales in comparison to what you are doing right now.

Do not get greedy

It is always better not to be too greedy in the case of a mutual fund. Sometimes people find the market is in upswing and they start to invest more and more. But it is very dangerous. Markets suddenly may fall and you may lose money. In the case of the long run, it is also not right. You should invest more when the market is down.

Do not panic

Sometimes investors become worried about their investments when the market goes downward; they forget their long-term objective and take such decisions that affect their long-term investment objectives.

Ignore the noise

You will find a lot of noise around your life. Sometimes noise is from the inside i.e. we started thinking about different parameters, start shifting our investments, and forget about our long-term goals. And sometimes noise is from the outside also. Some people or friends may talk about some fund, and we shift all our investments accordingly. We don't rely on our knowledge, our own analysis, or our own investment objectives. We should always understand the financial goal of every person is different.

Chasing high return in the short term

Sometimes we get attracted by short term high return and put money in this fund. We don't do any further analysis.

Investing in too many funds

It is also one of the mistakes which leads us in a difficult situation. We sometimes choose too many funds in our portfolios. It becomes too difficult to monitor our portfolios when we invest in too many funds, so always choose a minimum number of funds in your portfolio.

Not reviewing

In some cases, we initially do a lot of market study. Then we decide to go with the fund and start investing. Or, by the influence of some advisor, we invest in a fund. But we totally forget to review our investment when we are investing. We should review our investment on a yearly frequency.

Abandoning investment midway

We sometimes stop our investments without a major reason. We just do so being influenced by others. That should not be done. Stick with the fund until you find a major reason to stop investing in this fund.

Investing in the regular plan

New investors often become victims of middle men, brokers or advisors. They invest in a regular plan with the help of those middlemen. They pay high commission to middlemen, as the bigger the investment amount, the bigger the commission. So it is always advisable to avoid those middlemen. It is always better to buy funds directly from the website of the fund house. It is always desirable to invest in the direct plan for profit maximization.

Unclear Investment goal

This is also a major problem with new investors. They don't have clear goals or investment objectives. They just start to invest as they have heard that mutual fund investments are good and it gives a high return. So they fumble in many situations and take wrong decisions on their investments. Every investor should have a clear investment goal.

Too much trading

In case of mutual fund investments sometimes we do too much trading. That means we shift from one fund to another fund randomly, which is also not desirable.

Shifting from diversified fund to index fund

After investing in a diversified fund for a few years we sometimes suddenly decide to shift into an index fund. This is also a mistake. If you see in the long run a maximum diversified fund has beaten index fund, it implies that an index fund is good for a grown economy.

CHAPTER 4

How to Select A Mutual Fund

When it comes to selecting a mutual fund, what are the main criteria that you look for? If you say a historical rate of return, then you are not alone. According to a study performed by the Investment Institute Company, approximately 75% of fund buyers use past performance as their most cited data on which mutual funds to buy. Only about a fourth of the participants stated that they bothered to review the loads charged by the fund. If this is your mindset right now, drop it. This is just one of the many reasons why the common investor doesn't fully maximize his/her yield.

Looking Past the Facade – Historical Performance

Our standard of looking at the past performance of mutual funds as the primary indicator of which one to buy into has negatively skewed our potential rate of return. Why? There are many reasons – for instance, because today's winners often become tomorrow's losers. Let us take a look at a few funds that have produced outstanding rates of returns before yielding mediocre results:

Apex Mid Cap Growth Fund (BMCGX) - This fund posted above-average returns before the year 2000, due to its high composition of technology-oriented stocks. Nonetheless, within a short time, the fund assets fell by 720%, one of the steepest falls within a one-year time-span. The fund wasn't able to recover over the next twelve years and has since liquidated, meaning that it has fully closed.

The Chicken Little Growth Fund – It's expected that a fund with such a name wouldn't perform well. The Chicken Little Growth Fund produced spectacular results within the first 12 months of its existence, posting returns of 41%. It earned the top spot in one-year rankings for large-cap funds. But the situation got worse over time after producing the one-year stellar return. Since 56% of the fund's assets were concentrated in three stocks (Apple, Caterpillar, and Advanced Micro Devices), the fund heavily relied on the performance of the three companies. When these three companies stagnated, the Chicken Little Growth Fund lacked the expenses necessary to continue operating. After just 16 months of existence, the fund was liquidated by the directors.

Fidelity Magellan Fund (FMAGX) - FMAGX was once regarded as one of the best mutual funds to buy in, and many people bought into the fund believing that it would consistently produce high returns. What they didn't know was that Peter Lynch, who is often regarded as the best mutual fund manager of all time, managed this fund between 1977 and 1990 to produce the best 20-year return of any mutual fund ever. Nevertheless, most people who invested in FMAGX were disappointed with the fund's average return after Lynch stepped down, yielding negative returns in comparison to Lynch's astounding annual return of 29.2%. The fund has still not recovered to where its peak once was.

All three of the funds above posted high returns at one point in their lifetimes but weren't able to reproduce their success over long periods of time. Each of the funds mentioned above fell due to different reasons. BMCGX invested primarily in technology-oriented stocks, which fell drastically due to the Dot-Com Bubble (also known as the Internet Bubble). During that period of time, technology stocks were overvalued, meaning that people bought them for more than it was valued. Due to the rapid rate of growth on technology stock, compounded with investors ignoring important return metrics such as the Price/Equity ratio, many companies weren't able to keep up with the growing prices of their own stock. This caused the collapse of technology stock, and ultimately the Apex Mid Growth Fund.

The downfall of the Chicken Little Growth Fund was primarily due to poor management skills. Not only did the fund manager demonstrate disinterest in seeing the fund succeed (the fund only held around 20 stock types which were updated once a year), but he also used money from the clients to pay off his own personal expenses.

FMAGX had a unique scenario due to the presence of former fund manager, Peter Lynch. Lynch had tremendous success with producing returns higher than the market, but he resigned on 1990. Ever since then, FMAGX has turned over multiple managers, none which show even the slightest resemblance to what Lynch accomplished within his years as a fund manager.

Many of the mutual funds that collapsed after posting above-average returns, such as BMCGX, are sector oriented. Sector funds invest solely in businesses that operate in a particular industry or "sector" of the economy. This leaves less room for diversification since the vast majority of assets owned by the fund belong to companies within one industry. Having all assets in one industry can be risky, especially if the industry isn't performing well.

In recent years (as of 2015), sector funds – specifically biotechnology has been producing astonishing rates of return. For instance, Fidelity Select Biotechnology Portfolio annually returned 40.45% between 2010 and 2015 and 63.71% over the last year. Due to the fund's outstanding return rates, it's a "hot" mutual fund for people to buy into. But from historical trends of high returning mutual funds, we also see points where it drops more than most other mutual funds. With high returns comes volatility, the concept that higher returning stocks are capable of greater variation - from the peak of returns to the trough of negative returns. My general rule is to avoid sector funds, mainly because of its attachment to only one industry, making it poorly diversified. Also, biotechnology companies heavily rely on the ability to produce new breakthrough products in order to increase their value. Theoretically, if the rate of producing new products decreases, or if there is a roadblock that prevents the industry from releasing their products to the public (i.e. scientists prove that genetically modified foods have negative effects on our health), then the troubles of the industry will also reflect itself onto the sector fund.

Will there be a crash just like the Dot-Com Bubble? It's generally a good idea to be cautious when investing in sector funds. If you want to invest in sector funds, make sure that only a small portion of your portfolio is allocated to it. Try to avoid hot funds that everyone is talking about, because they have historically been shown to be susceptible to crashes.

Before you start ignoring historical performances all together due to what was discussed in the previous section, it's important that you know that past performances can be a good indicator in how a mutual fund is doing when combined with other analytical data. If you have a mutual fund that has been consistently producing lower returns than other mutual funds of the same benchmark, then you may have to consider switching funds. However, note that the mutual fund in question should be regularly posting below average results (i.e. 1.5 to 2 years). Short term performance reductions can be due to a few bad investment choices, which can be overturned.

Know your objectives and risk tolerance

Prior to buying mutual fund shares, you should determine the desires and objectives that you want to achieve. Are you looking for long-term profits? Are you satisfied with your current income? Are you planning to use your money for college expenses? Do you want to store away your money so you can use it once you retire?

You also need to think about your tolerance against risks. Are you willing to risk your money in aggressive financial ventures? Which levels of losses are acceptable for you? Do you want the financial manager to handle your funds conservatively?

Determine the investment style and type of mutual fund suitable for you – If you are planning to invest your money for a long period of time and are willing to face considerable risks, then you should look for a "long-term investment appreciation" fund. Mutual fund companies that belong to this type often invest their funds in the stock market. That is why they are considered as volatile mutual funds.

If you want quick profits, on the other hand, you should purchase shares from an "income" fund. These mutual fund companies often focus on corporate liabilities and government debts.

Check the fees and charges

Mutual fund companies earn income by charging fees to their investors. Because of this, you have to completely understand the different fees that you may encounter.

Some companies charge a "load fee," which is basically a transaction fee applied upon the acquisition or sale of an investment. The fees applied during acquisition are called "front-end load fees" while the ones applied during a sale are called "back-end load fees." These fees are usually 4% to 6% of the investment's total value. Mutual fund companies apply these fees to cover the management charges related to the investment and to discourage client turnovers.

In general, you should look for "no-load" mutual fund companies. These companies don't require their investors to pay back-end or front-end fees. On the other hand, they may charge other types of fees (e.g. administration fees, management expense ratio, etc.).

Identify the size of the company:

In general, the mutual fund company's size doesn't hamper its capacity to earn profits. However, there are certain situations where the company gets too big. Fidelity's Magellan Fund is a great example for this. The large inflows into the company's capital forced it to modify its investment strategies and processes. As a result, it experienced a significant decline in terms or performance and profitability.

Avoiding Loads and High Expenses

You may have heard of the terminologies like "no-load" or "operating expenses" when referring to mutual funds. What do they mean? Loads are basically a short term way of saying sales charge or commission. When you purchase into a fund through a brokerage, the broker takes a small portion of the money as compensation for being the medium, and for his/her time spent selecting an appropriate fund for the client. Load rates are usually around 3-8% (most commonly at 3 – 5.75%), which means that if you invest $1,000 into the fund, $30-$80 will be taken as commission. If a fund has no loads, it simply means that fund company directly offers the mutual fund to the public, thereby passing the brokerage intermediary. Fund investors should understand that loads are sales charges associated with only the financial intermediary, not the actual fund company itself. Do not purchase load funds believing that your funds will perform better than everyone else's, even if a brokerage firm tells you otherwise.

Mutual fund operating expenses, or simply just "fees and expenses" are the associated costs with running a mutual fund.

This may include the fund manager's salary, setting up customer service, filing and mailing prospectuses, etc. There is no way to avoid operating expenses, because every business needs expenses to provide goods and services. However, some funds charge more expenses than others. What you want is to maximize the difference between annual returns and expenses. Typically, expenses are charged annually from the total amount of assets you have in the fund. For example, if the total amount that you have acquired in the fund is $10,000, and the fund charges an annual expense of 2%, $200 would be deducted from your assets.

What is important is that you keep in mind that both loads and expenses can be detrimental to your fund's long term rate of return, especially if you keep on buying and selling your funds (which I don't recommend). Just imagine a scenario where you contribute $10,000 to a mutual fund, with front and back load ends of 4%. Say that you're looking to withdraw all your money in 20 years and that the fund's average rate of return was 8%. When you buy into the fund, $400 will be deducted from your contribution by the front-end load, leaving $9,600 for the fund manager to use in investments. If we have a 2% total expense ratio, your assets by the end of the 20-year span will have accumulated to approximately $30,788. You won't have to worry about the back-end load though, since you've likely passed your load's holding period, which is the total amount of time held onto your assets (load percentage decreases over time). Now imagine the exact same scenario without loads and a total expense ratio of 1%. You contribute $10,000 into the fund, compounded at 8% per year. The assets will be priced at $38,697 by the end of a 20-year span. Which fund would you rather buy into?

Now, you may say that funds with loads and higher expense ratios perform better, but that's not true at all. For one, it has been shown in a multitude of studies that the presence of a load does not affect the performance of the fund in any way whatsoever. After all, loads are part of the brokerage, not the fund company. Buying load funds only open up the opportunities that brokerages offer, which have no impact whatsoever on the performance of the fund. Expense ratios are just the same. In fact, it has been shown that funds with higher expense ratios actually produce lower returns. Why? Because the higher expense ratio offsets the performance of the fund. If the fund charges 1% more on expense than other funds, then it will have to produce 1% higher returns on average than these other funds, which is usually not the case. In other words, most funds with higher expenses aren't able to produce enough extra returns to offset the expense.

Best Fund Companies

Finding the "best" is always a subjective exercise. There are tens of thousands of fund options out there, so how do you know which will be the best for you? Surprisingly, the better-known companies such as Fidelity Investments and Vanguard offer some of the best funds. When I say "best," I usually mean stable, no loads funds that offer good average return rates. Now, let's go straight to analyze top-notch fund companies. Note that some companies may or may not be listed.

Fidelity Investments- Fidelity is one of the largest mutual fund companies in the United States and well known for being a provider of retirement services, such as company managed 401(k) and individual retirement plans. It's a public firm owned by shareholders, which typically means that their goal is to maximize growth and returns. This is among the major explanations why there are so many more Fidelity advertisements than other large fund companies, such as Vanguard. Fidelity has a wide variety of actively managed funds, but primarily specializes in retirement funds performance-wise. Also, please take note that Fidelity funds are not always load-free.

Vanguard- Vanguard offers a broad spectrum of funds that range in risks, but they are pretty consistent when it comes to managing these funds intelligently. They do not take unnecessary risks, which often translates to lower volatility than many other non-Vanguard funds, but also never performing with the best of funds. However, do not overlook this! As I've stated earlier, the best performing funds today can be the worst funds tomorrow. Vanguard specializes in bond funds performance-wise, but also offers many other types of funds that have low expense ratios.

And best of yet, Vanguard funds do not have loads tacked onto them.

T. Rowe Price- Like Fidelity Investments and Vanguard, T. Rowe Price is also one of the premier fund companies in the United States. T. Rowe Price primarily specializes in domestic-equity funds, with all but a few claiming bronze rankings or above in Morningstar (a renowned investor resource website). The area of weakness is international equity funds, so I would tend to avoid those if you plan on investing in T. Rowe Price.

Dodge & Cox - Dodge & Cox is a firm based in San Francisco. It has been around for a long time – since the Great Depression. Dodge and Cox are primarily known for its conservative funds with great, solid track records.

The four fund companies listed above are examples of good investment firms that you should consider. They often offer fair expense ratios, and only a few of the funds have loads tacked on. Many people use these four mutual fund firms, which saturates the fund and allows for greater diversification.

Turnover and Taxes

Turnover ratio and your income tax bracket are two factors that you should also consider when purchasing into a mutual fund. Turnover ratio is the percentage of assets within the fund that has been "overturned," or replaced with other holdings in a given year. If the fund that you are in has a turnover ratio of 100%, then that means the assets within the fund have been bought and sold on average once per year. The turnover ratio largely relies on the fund manager's investment strategy, but take note that it can affect your overall post-tax returns. Fund investors often skip by details such as turnover ratio, going for the fund that yields the highest returns. However, taxes play in a big role in the amount of money you can put in your pocket. For example, a fund can return 12.23% before taxes. The return after tax distributions could be 9.37% after factoring the amount earned from withdrawing capital gains and dividends. If your investments are in a retirement account, you can breathe a sigh of relief from the tax burdens, but do not overlook the volatility of mutual funds with a high turnover ratio.

Not only does the turnover ratio impact your post-tax returns, but it also clouds the mutual fund's long term perspective. If you have a fund that constantly buys and sells the assets that it owns, you cannot get a general feel for what the fund is investing in. This can be detrimental to your overall return in the long term, as the fund can alter drastically and stray from its initial objective.

Dangers associated with market timing

Market timing happens the moment an investor attempts to predict the direction of the market – whether a particular stock or bond will rise or fall in price. Ever since the creation of the stock market, investors have been trying to predict the movements of the market by reading numerous articles and annual statements provided by companies. In recent years, people have shifted to using complicated software that attempts to foretell the direction of the stock market, ultimately with little success. One thing to remember: do not attempt to time the market. This is especially true if you do not have years of experience behind you. If you short sell during times where you believe that the market will fall, you have the potential to lose a lot of money if it doesn't go the way that you want it to.

Another reason why you shouldn't market time is that your prediction has to be right not once, but twice. You risk getting out after a severe drop, missing a big market comeback, and jumping back in only to experience another loss. In this scenario, you would end up much worse off than if you simply just left your assets alone.

CHAPTER 5

The Buying and Selling Process of Mutual Fund Shares

S hares can be bought directly from the mutual fund company. Insurance agents, financial planners, banks, and brokers also sell mutual fund shares. Mutual fund companies buy back the shares from any investor who wants to sell them. Payment is usually made within 7 days. The value of a mutual fund share can easily be known by calling the mutual fund company or by checking its website. Some major newspapers also print the net asset value of various mutual fund companies. An investor who wants to buy mutual fund shares checks the net asset value per share because this is the basis of the purchase price. In most cases, he also has to pay a purchase fee or a purchase sales load. If he wants to sell his shares, he also has to take note of the net asset value. He will receive the amount based on the net asset value less any other fees, like redemption fee or deferred sales load. The net asset value (NAV) of the mutual fund fluctuates every trading day. Also, you can know the value of your shares by visiting the fund's website or calling its toll-free number. You can also find NAVs for various mutual funds from the major newspapers.

When buying the shares, you will need to pay the current NAV per share on top of any fees that the fund will assess at the time of purchase. These might include purchase sales load fee and other types of purchase fees.

When selling your shares, the fund will pay you the NAV less any fee the fund will assess at the time of sale. Some of these fees might include back end fees, sales load, or redemption fees. Remember, the fund's NAV goes up and down as its holdings change in value. The process is simplified as shown in the figure below

Exchange of Mutual Fund Shares

Mutual funds can form a group known as "family of funds." These funds usually share distribution and administrative systems even though each fund has its own strategies and objectives. Each fund within the family can be exchanged thereby providing investors the privilege to move their investments from one fund to another. An investor takes advantage of it when his risk tolerance or investment goals change. Most funds within the family don't charge fees for the transfer. Before deciding to move the investment within the family of funds, the investor must check for tax consequences. He may need to pay capital gains tax.

How an Investor Earns from Mutual Funds

An investor can earn money from mutual funds through dividend payments, capital gains distribution, and increased net asset value. The interest and dividends on the securities are distributed by the fund to its investors by giving out dividends as well. Furthermore, any capital gain from the securities is also distributed to the investors. Lastly, the investor earns if there is an increase in the net asset value of the fund. In most cases, the mutual fund company lets the investor choose if he'll receive the dividends and capital gains in cash or they get reinvested to the fund.

The explanation on how an investor earns money is as discussed below:

Through payment of dividends and interests

You can earn money from your fund in the form of dividends and interests generated by your portfolio. The fund will then pay you all the income minus the disclosed expenses it has earned as dividends.

Through capital gains distribution

The price of securities owned by the fund may increase. This way, the fund will realize a capital gain when it sells portfolios that have risen in price. At the end of the financial year, the fund may distribute these capital gains to shareholders.

Increase in NAV

If the market value of the fund's portfolio rises, after taking away the expenses and liabilities, then NAV of the fund and its shares will rise. Higher NAV indicates a rise in the value of your investment. When it comes to distribution of capital gains and payment of dividends, the fund will always give you two choices. You can request your cash, or you can reinvest the dividends or distributions back by buying more shares. However, you will not pay any additional sales load.

How to Make Money in Mutual Funds through Dividends

Dividends are simply the amount of money that is being given to the shareholders of a fund in regular periods of time. This dividend will depend on how much money the company made divided by shares of stock, or shares in the mutual fund.

The time may differ from one fund to another, but shareholders are usually given dividends either every month or every quarter of the year.

How to Make Money in Mutual Funds through Capital Appreciation

Capital appreciation is also called capital gains. This simply means that the value of the mutual fund portfolio rises as a direct result of the prevailing economy and market conditions. Since the value of the mutual fund portfolio rises, your investment in said mutual fund also rises.

Take note of the concept of paper loss and paper gain with respect to mutual fund investment. To put it simply, paper gain means that the level of the mutual fund portfolio rises without the financial managers selling the current investment position.

If paper gains are the case, there is still a possibility that the mutual fund portfolio and your investment will plummet. Conversely, a paper loss means that the level of the mutual fund portfolio plummets without the financial managers selling the current investment position.

A paper loss means that there is still a possibility that the mutual fund portfolio will recover once the prevailing economy and market conditions become favorable.

How to Make Money in Mutual Funds through an Increase in the Net Asset Value (NAV)

In order to compute for the (NAV), you will simply subtract the present value of the liabilities of the mutual fund from the present value of the mutual fund portfolio. After which, you will divide the result by the number of the shares outstanding.

Fees and Charges of the Mutual Fund

Remember that your mutual fund company is a business too. This means that they need to profit from their services to you and the other investors. As such, these mutual fund companies will always have costs, charges, and fees that they will impose on investors in order to make the operation profitable.

You must understand all of these costs, fees, and charges in order to make an informed decision of the mutual fund to invest in. After all, remember that all these costs, charges, and fees lower the returns of your investments. At the end of the day, perform your due diligence or you may end up paying much more than you need to and earning very little or even losing for your efforts.

Shareholder Fees and Charges

Sales load/Sales Charge on Purchases/Front end load

This refers to the cash you pay to the mutual fund in order to invest.

It is vital to put into contemplation that under present law on securities (of the USA), the sales load cannot be higher than 8.5% of the total amount of the investment of a shareholder.

The most common rate of sales load is set to 5%. This means that if you intend to invest $2,000 in your chosen Mutual Fund, you will pay a sales load of $100. Conversely, if you intend to invest $4,000, the sales load that you will incur is $200.

Deferred sales load/Deferred sales charge/Back end load

This refers to the cash you pay to the mutual fund or broker when you sell the shares that you presently own.

The rate of the deferred sales load is typically dependent on the time that you have invested in the mutual fund.

The universal rule is, the more you have invested in the mutual fund, the lower the deferred sales load that you will have to pay.

Annual Expenses on Operations

Management fees - This refers to the fees that are derived from the assets of the mutual fund portfolio as a form of compensation for the services of the financial and money managers.

Expense Ratio/Total annual fund operating expenses- This refers to the table of fees that outlines all the expenses of the mutual fund company. It is simplified as a percentage of the assets of the mutual fund portfolio. This is a very helpful guide for prospective investors when it comes to comparing one mutual fund company to another

Selling of Mutual Fund Shares

A lot of investors are often tempted to sell back their mutual fund shares to the company if the fund yielded a lower return. Some investments may have a higher return, so these investors are enticed to move their investments. It is perfectly fine to move the money to an investment with a higher yield. However, investors must first know about liquidating his shares, as he may suffer negative consequences if the sale of the investment isn't made right.

A mutual fund isn't the same as stock. The stock market may decline but it doesn't mean that the investor has to sell his fund shares. Investors, who invest in stocks, often find themselves in a state of panic when the price of a stock falls. They decide to sell the stock to cash in on their gains or minimize losses.

A mutual fund, on the other hand, isn't like a single stock. It is a portfolio of various investments like bonds and stocks which are chosen by the fund or portfolio manager. In short, a mutual fund is a diversified portfolio, although each fund has its own degree of diversification. A balanced fund is the most diversified while the sector fund is the least. A decline in one or 2 stocks isn't going to have a great effect on the whole fund. As a diversified portfolio, an investor can't rely on market timing alone if he wants to sell his fund shares. Furthermore, the rate of return of a mutual fund may improve over time.

Factors to Consider in Selling Mutual Fund Shares

An investor who has mutual fund shares which charges a back-end load can expect to receive less money when he sells his shares. If the mutual fund charges a front-end load, the sales fees were already deducted at the time the investment was made. Most mutual funds would charge a higher back-end load if the shares were sold early. If the realized capital gains were significant, the investor might be asked to pay capital gains tax. If the shares were redeemed at a higher price, he would also be asked to pay capital gains tax.

What Happens When There is a Change in the Mutual Fund

An investor who has decided to keep the mutual fund for a long term need not keep it if there are significant changes to the fund, which can have a damaging effect to the investment. In general, the mutual fund is supposed to maximize the investment in order to grow the wealth of an investor over time. Its purpose is not to make the investor loyal to the fund.

An investor who buys shares in a mutual fund is actually putting his trust to the knowledge and expertise of the fund manager. He is hoping that the fund manager can generate an outstanding return on his investment. If there's a change in the fund manager, the investor must pay attention. If it's an index fund, the investor need not worry because the fund isn't actively managed. However, if it's some other type of mutual fund, the mutual fund company must let its investors know the reason for the fund manager change. It is good practice to research the performance and experience of the new fund manager.

An investor who did his research prior to investing in a mutual fund must have chosen a fund which meets his needs and goals. As such, if the mutual fund suddenly makes investments in financial products which run contrary to the original goals of the mutual fund, the investor may reevaluate his holdings in the fund. Furthermore, some mutual funds may change names in order to entice more investors to sign up with them. Some funds also change strategies to go with the change in name. An investor who is bothered by such changes can sell back his shares to the fund.

In general, it's not good to sell back mutual fund shares if the fund underperforms in less than a year. The fund may just be experiencing fluctuations over a short term. However, if the fund underperforms for 2 consecutive years, it is best to sell the shares to minimize further losses. The performance of the fund can also suffer if it becomes too big. In general, it becomes harder to manage the fund if it becomes bigger. This problem is often magnified if the fund is a small-cap fund or focused fund.

If there's a change in the investor's portfolio, there may be a need to sell the mutual fund shares in order to move the money to a better portfolio. An investor may adhere to an asset allocation model. So, he may sell his shares in order to rebalance his portfolio and bring it back to the original. He may also purchase more mutual fund shares if he wants. Furthermore, investment goals may change. Thus, he may also plan on rebalancing his investment portfolio. Lastly, the investor may sell his shares to take advantage of tax breaks due to major capital losses suffered by the mutual fund. Such a tax break may offset the profits gained from other investments.

The Costs of A Mutual Fund

Mutual funds also have costs involved like distribution expenses, marketing expenses, investment advisory fees, and investor transaction costs. These costs are passed on to investors. Therefore, it is important for new investors to know that they may have lower returns because they will have to pay some fees.

A shareholder fee is charged by some mutual funds when an investor transacts shares with the company. Furthermore, operating expenses are also shouldered by each investor because these expenses are paid from the fund. The Exchange Commission and securities require each mutual fund to make known every expense and fee it collects through a fee table which is printed in the prospectus of each fund.

A front-end load is charged by a mutual fund to an investor who purchases shares. This amount goes to the pocket of the broker who facilitated the purchase. This means that the front-end load reduces the investor's investment to the mutual fund. The front-end load is limited to 8.5% of the investment. In the United States of America, this cap is set by FINRA. The purchase fee is charged by some mutual funds when an investor buys shares of the fund. It differs from the front-end load because it is paid directly to the fund and not to the broker. It is often collected to pay for the associated costs of the purchase.

A deferred sales charge is a fee paid by the investor when he sells his mutual fund shares. Its other name is back-end load. The money goes to the broker who facilitated the transaction. In most cases, the amount is dependent on the length of time the investor held the shares. It could be zero if he had his mutual fund shares for a long time. A redemption fee, on the other hand, is an amount collected by the fund from an investor who wants to sell his shares. It goes to the fund to cover the expenses incurred in processing the sale.

An exchange fee is an amount collected from a shareholder who wants to move his investment to another mutual fund within the family of funds while an account fee is charged to shareholders for their account's maintenance.

A management fee is an amount deducted from the fund assets to pay for the investment adviser of the mutual fund while a distribution fee is an amount taken out from the fund to pay for selling shares, marketing, and other investor services. It includes the amount paid to brokers for helping sell the mutual fund shares. The shareholder service fee is also part of the distribution fee. It is an amount paid to the mutual fund staff to reply to investor queries. On the other hand, other expenses include administrative expenses, transfer agent expenses, accounting and legal expenses, custodial fees, and other fees not included in the fees discussed earlier.

A no-load fund doesn't pay brokers to buy and sell transactions of investors. However, it may charge other fees like account fees, exchange fees, redemption fees, and purchase fees. This mutual fund also has operating expenses. A new investor must consider every fee being charged by the mutual fund. In fact, he should compute the fees charges because even a small fee can accumulate and become substantial over time.

There are mutual funds which charge lower front-end loads if the investor's investment is substantial. A breakpoint is that level of investment which is eligible for a lower sales load. Although the Securities and Exchange Commission doesn't require mutual funds to offer breakpoints, the SEC requires those mutual funds which offer them to disclose them as well. Furthermore, FINRA doesn't permit brokers to sell shares below the breakpoint for the purpose of earning higher commissions.

There is really no standard formula in calculating a breakpoint. Each mutual fund company derives its own computation. Therefore, an investor must ask the fund company how it computes eligibility for a breakpoint. Costs make the investor's return lower. Furthermore, most mutual funds have sub-par performance because of these costs. Some of these funds even hide their costs using complex jargons and computations. Thus, critics say that these companies tend to confuse their investors with all these fees. Basically, fees fall under 2 categories: recurring annual fees and transaction fees.

The Expense-Ratio

The expense ratio also, known as management expense ratio, represents all recurring annual expenses. The management expense ratio includes the hiring cost, the investment manager, administrative costs, and the 12b-1 fee. The cost of hiring an investment manager ranges between percentages of 0.5% to 1%. Although this may be a small percentage, it can amount to millions if the fund is substantial. However, investors mustn't believe that a high fee equates to better fund performance. Administrative costs include customer service, record keeping, postage, etc. There are mutual funds which minimize these costs. However, not all of these funds are excellent in keeping the costs down. Finally, the 12b-1 fee in the United States of America is a recurring cost. It pays for promotions, advertising, and broker commissions. In general, an index fund only has an expense ratio of 0.2% while the average expense ratio of an equity mutual fund can go up to 1.5%. An international fund or specialty fund charges a higher expense ratio because these finds require a highly experienced fund manager.

CHAPTER 6

Tips to Ensure that Your Mutual Funds are Profitable

A highlight of what to expect in this chapter includes the following:

Essential 1st tip - Be Very Careful with the Mutual Fund's Expense Ratio

Essential 2nd tip - Do Not Invest in Mutual Funds with High Turnover Ratios

Essential 3rd tip - Your Mutual Funds Must Have a Disciplined, Knowledgeable and Experienced Money Management Team

Essential 4th tip - Your Mutual Funds Must Have Sufficient Asset Diversification

Essential 5th tip - Dollar Cost Average

Tip 1: Be Very Careful with the Mutual Funds' Expense Ratio

As explained in the previous section, expense ratio refers to the expenses regularly incurred by the mutual fund company for its operations and even the salaries of the professional money management team. The expenses incurred from operations include the activities that you utilize. These include the following: organization of the shareholder's meetings, electricity and other utility bills, rent or lease for the office, management fees, costs for the fliers and reports, the salaries of the mutual fund agents, sales loads, and even the coffee that they served you from the moment you sign up with them. Imagine, you have to pay all these things even before you invest in the mutual fund itself.

In other words, the mutual fund's expense ratio is the cost that you incur for owning a share in the mutual fund. As such, it will be important to take into consideration that before you can even start earning money from your investments, the mutual fund company must first break even with the expense ratio (expenses that they incurred prior your investment).

Therefore, you must look for a mutual fund that has the lowest expense ratio as possible. As an illustrative example, suppose that you are looking at two mutual funds for your investment. The first mutual fund has a 1.5% expense ratio while the second has a 0.16% expense ratio. Clearly, if you chose the first mutual fund with a 1.5% expense ratio, it will be more difficult for you to earn money through your investments. Suppose that you invested $10,000 for 10 years in both investment funds. According to recent research, over that span of 10 years, note that your expense ratios for the first mutual fund will be around $1,800 while your expense ratios for the second mutual fund will be around $230. In essence, it would be very valuable for you to choose a mutual fund that has a low expense ratio.

Tip 2: Do Not Invest in Mutual Funds with High Turnover Ratios

It will also be important for you to avoid mutual funds with high turnover ratios. To put it simply, turnover ratios refer to the certain percentage of the mutual fund portfolio that is being sold and bought for every calendar year.

Now the question is this: Why are the turnover ratio or rates bad in the first place? Taxes. Take note that, for every transaction of the mutual fund portfolio – whether it is to buy or sell a security – the fund will pay taxes.

Imagine there are two mutual fund companies – mutual fund X and mutual fund Y. For both mutual funds, you have invested a total of $10,000 for a span of 10 years. Mutual fund X has 18% growth rate annually for the past 10 years but has 100% turnover rate. On the other hand, Mutual fund Y has a growth rate of 12% annually with no turnover at all. Which do you think is the mutual fund that is more profitable? The answer is Mutual fund Y. Remember that the more turnover your mutual fund company does, the more taxes your fund (and hard earned money) will pay. As such, even though Mutual fund X has a higher return, it pays more taxes for every turnover it commits. This will significantly diminish your returns. On the other hand, Mutual Fund Y does not even pay a single penny in taxes for the last 10 years. As such, Mutual Fund Y has the superior amount of money after taxes.

There are even mutual fund companies out there that have 50% or more turnover rates. This will be a terrible proposition for any kind of mutual fund investor. The best thing to do is to avoid these kinds of mutual fund companies at all costs!

Of course, the only exception to this rule is if taxes are not a concern for you. The truth is, the situation is different from one person to another. However, the general public will definitely pay taxes. As such, by and large, investors will pay taxes.

However, there are people who will not. Are there any people who are not concerned with taxes? Yes there are. These people are already investing through a tax-free account. These are investment accounts that include your Roth IRA, Traditional IRA and 401 (k) under the USA jurisdiction.

Tip 3: Your Mutual Funds Must Have a Disciplined, Knowledgeable and Experienced Money Management Team

At the end of the day, it will be your hard earned money that will be at stake when it comes to the performance of your chosen mutual fund. As such, it would be important to pick a mutual fund company that is composed of competent, disciplined, knowledgeable, and experienced money managers. With the level of technology today, it would very easy to look at the background of the money managers of the mutual fund company you are looking in. Take advantage of the information in blogs, forums, online readers, reviews, and even social networking sites.

Should you discover that some of the money managers in the mutual fund company have bad track records or a terrible history performance (i.e., losses) for the investors' portfolios, the most sensible thing to do is to avoid that company altogether.

Among the ways in which you can control the devotion of the money managers in the performance of the mutual fund itself is they must have substantial capital invested in the said mutual fund to control it. This way, you can be comfortable in the fact that the money managers have also risked their capital in the mutual fund alongside yours. This means that if the mutual fund succeeds, the money managers will get wealthy (if not more wealthy!). On the other hand, if the mutual fund fails, they will also lose their capital.

Tip 4: Your Mutual Funds Must Have Sufficient Asset Diversification

Diversification is a good method for making sure that you are not exposed to unnecessary risks such as industry or company risk. The reason is that over-concentration of a portfolio in a specific company or industry (the direct opposite of diversification) opens or exposes you to a great amount of risk. If the company you have solely invested on becomes bankrupt, your hard earned money will perish!

According to Warren Buffett, one of the wealthiest people in the planet, diversification of assets is the most potent method for people who do not have enough time to study the markets full time. Supposed you are thinking of investing in a mutual fund, chances are you are one of those people who do not have enough time to study the markets that Warren Buffett cited. As such, it would make sense to practice diversification in your mutual fund portfolio. Listed below are the key concepts of diversification that will help your mutual fund investments very profitable:

- Avoid owning mutual funds that have a portfolio that relies heavily on a specific industry.

- Choose mutual funds that spread the portfolio assets out to different companies across all types of industries.

- Pick a mutual fund that invests across all types of assets such as real estate, fixed income funds, arbitrage, and international funds.

Tip 5: The Dollar Cost Average

This tip is a strategy that is often used by investors through the act of buying securities (stocks, bonds, real estate, foreign exchange, mutual funds, money market funds, etc.) in amounts and time intervals that are already predetermined. By preparing a clear and distinct plan in your investments, you will be able to save enormous time, money and effort.

To put it simply, in dollar cost averaging, you will invest a certain amount of cash into security (stocks, bonds, real estate, foreign exchange, mutual funds, money market funds, etc.) for regular intervals of time instead of outright investments of a lump sum.

Without a doubt, the most profitable way to invest in mutual funds is to dollar cost average! Of all the possible profitable strategies in mutual funds investing, dollar cost averaging is the most fundamentally sound because of two reasons:

- By dollar cost averaging your investments, you will be able to lower your overall cost over time!

- By dollar cost averaging your investments, you will be able to significantly diminish your investment and market risk especially when you intend to invest for the long term!

Now that you know the benefits of dollar cost averaging your investments in mutual funds, the question you might ask is this: How do I implement this strategy in my mutual funds' portfolio? You just have to follow this 5-step quick and easy guide:

- Decide on the regular time interval that you will be able to invest. Will you invest every month, every quarter or every six months? According to studies, investing every month is the best way to form the habit of saving and investing!

- Regulate the amount of cash that you will be able to invest for every quarter, every six months or every month. This money may come from your salary or from any of your passive income sources (if any). For example, you may decide to devote $500 every month to your mutual funds' portfolio. If you can devote more, then that would be better!

- Decide that you would commit at least 5 years of your money in investing in mutual funds. According to research on wealth and finance, the best way to invest in pooled funds such as mutual funds is by investing for the long term (10 years and above).

- Select a mutual fund that is perfect for your needs, goals and investing temperament.

- Every month, quarter or six months, invest the money in your chosen mutual funds! If you can, set up an automatic withdrawal plan with your broker. It is important to note that there are a lot of brokers in the United States that offer their clients an option to automatically withdraw money from their accounts to invest in the mutual fund in your chosen time intervals. In this way, the process of investing in mutual funds becomes automated. As such, there would be less hassle and effort on your part when it comes to investing. The figure below illustrates more on this tip

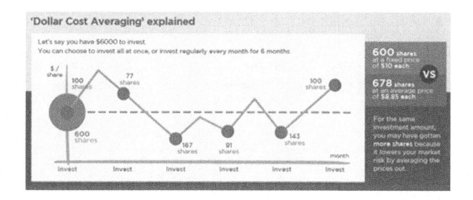

CHAPTER 7

Retirement Income Planning on Mutual Funds

When willing to invest in mutual funds for Supplemental Retirement Income Planning, you have a large number of options. It is essential to constantly break down the arrangement, its confinements, and the dangers you will run. In this way, it would be less demanding for you to limit your options. For this issue, it could be useful to get in contact with a Retirement Income Planning monetary expert.

Mutual funds are characterized in three principle classifications that vary with respect to their dangers, highlights and rewards. They are currency showcase reserves, security reserves, which likewise get the name of "settled salary" lastly, stock assets, which are additionally called "value reserves."

Currency Market Funds can just invest into simply some great, here and now speculation that be issued by the U.S. government, U.S. companies, and nearby governments. These assets endeavor to keep the estimation of an offer in reserve, called the net resource esteem (NRE) at a stable $1.00 an offer. The profits for these assets have dependably been lower than the other two sorts of assets. Along these lines, currency advertises that reserves investors must know about the "swelling risk." In spite of the fact that Bond Funds are somewhat unsafe than currency advertises, more often than not, dangers can be controlled with more prominent conviction than stocks. Moreover, because of the way that there are numerous sorts of Bond Funds, their dangers and prizes fluctuate extraordinarily. These dangers may envelop credit chance, which alludes to the likelihood that backers whose securities are claimed by the reserve don't pay their obligations; or loan cost risk and prepayment chance, which is related to the possibility that a bond is "resigned" early. At long last, there are contrasts between one stock reserve and another. For example, Growth Funds are centered around stocks that give extensive capital additions, Income Funds invest into stocks that compensation ordinary profits, and Sector Funds are had practical experience specifically industry portions. As a rule, they present a medium-to-abnormal state of risk.

Along these lines, individuals who are intending to invest into a store that consolidates development and pay, which are unquestionably key variables, may discover common subsidizes a fascinating adjusted elective decision for Supplemental Retirement Income Planning.

Retirement Planning

Plan your retirement for income through mutual fund investment.

A large portion of the general population has not made arrangements for their retirement. As it's been said, *"the future is capricious and we have to live in the present' however my dear companion's future is the result of the present, our present will choose our future."* When we consider retirement, we by and large consider maturity, a period when you need to surrender the activity and sit at home doing nothing. In spite of the reality, a large portion of the retiree carries on with exceptionally dynamic lifestyles. We have to genuinely consider our retirement arrangements on the grounds that, once we retire and the salary is no more, we still meet all our daily expenses.

In such manner, shared stores have ended up being the correct response for making retirement arranging less demanding and more secure. The common store being overseen by experts is a key to viable retirement arranging.

A few people like it. A few people don't know, however, that the truth of the matter is that retirement is a reality for each working individual. Most youngsters today assume they cannot consider retirement as a reality because they have that notion of in "living at present." Nonetheless, it is essential to get ready for your post-retirement life in the event that you wish to hold your monetary freedom and keep up an agreeable way of life. This is critical, in light of the fact that, in contrast to created countries, India does not have a standardized savings net. In India, individuals still rely on bank investment funds and settled stores for retirement reasons, which is sadly lacking.

Basically, retirement arranging implies ensuring you will have enough money to live on in the wake of resigning from work. Retirement ought to be the best time of your life. To accomplish a problem-free resigned life, you have to settle on reasonable venture choices amid your working life, giving your well-deserved money something to do for you in the future.

Despite the fact that the necessary investment funds in provident reserves through both representative and investors commitments should offer some padding, it may not be sufficient to help you all through your retirement. That is the reason retirement arranging is critical for everyone. Moreover, with shared subsidizes, the financial specialists can really get ready for themselves and accomplish their intended goals. When contrasted with direct values, this choice of shared store is significantly more secure for arranging your retirement.

Getting ready for retirement is as essential as arranging your vocation or marriage. We have to take cognizant and cautious choices to get ready for our retirement. The lifestyle takes its own course and from the poorest to the wealthiest, each one gets more established with time. We get more seasoned each day, without figuring it out. With our coming maturity, we have a tendency to wind up all the more understanding to the unavoidable issues facing everyone and understand the significance and effect of retirement. The future depends on the decisions you make today.

Retirement arrangement implies ensuring you will have enough money to live on after leaving your work. Retirement is that time of your life when you can take a load off. Retirement ought to get a greater amount of satisfaction your life by receiving rewards of what you gain in such a large number of long stretches of the work done during employment. The bigger part of the general population moves on with their noticeably bad life at retirement.

This is a no-commitment, free shared store warning; financial specialists can settle on educated mutual fund venture choices with the help of our counselors.

SIP - Systematic Investment Plan

It is a monthly plan where you invest a fixed amount of money in the mutual fund of your choice. The monthly investment causes the buying of stocks at all market levels, causing your stock buying to be averaged.

For example, you would gain maximum if you buy a stock at the absolute bottom, that is when its price is very low. But, you may not judge the absolute bottom of a stock. For this reason, you keep investing a small amount every month to average your buying price. This safeguards the investor from expensive buying.

If you have knowledge of stock markets, and you are confident about your view of stock market conditions, then you may also put a large sum of money in mutual funds, as "Lump Sum." This has the advantage of getting you stocks at a cheap rate, but only if you are right. If you are wrong in timing the market, then you will end up paying a lot more as compared to SIP.

In reality, even individuals with quite a lot of experience are not in a position to track the share trading system elements, subsequently falling prey to bad choices. Well-established securities exchange contributing technique is something that individuals consider to be good. It is something that can be pursued, but, however, can most likely never be accomplished.

In any case, is it the right idea? Are things like destiny, luckiness, shot, and so on the integral factors in money market ventures? Or, on the other hand, is there any way to approach the share trading system in a theoretical way?

The response to the above inquiry most likely lies in the Systematic Investment Plan or SIP (a.k.a. "Occasional Payment Plan" or "Authoritative Plan").

The Systematic Investment Plan (SIP), unlike the one-time venture designs, involves standard installments for a settled period. It enables financial specialists to accumulate offers of a shared reserve by contributing a settled (which is frequently little) measure of money all the time. What's more, it offers the accompanying support points promptly appealing to any financial analyst. The SIP has the following measures:

Decreased weight on your tote – Through SIP, you can enter money markets even with doubts. Your failure to contribute a fat sum may has kept you from putting resources into money markets.

Working for the future – We have certain requirements that can be intended for long ventures. Such needs incorporate youngsters' instruction, purchasing your very own place, post-retirement crises, and so on. Furthermore, SIP offers valuable help in such a manner. It causes you to spare a little sum all the time. Also, in due time it transforms into a generous sum.

Mixes returns – SIP does not encourage you to achieve a considerable sum after a specific timeframe. You can achieve that sum at an early age, depending on when you begin contributing. You can gather a prominent sum at 70 on the off chance that you begin contributing at 35. A prior begin at 25 can empower you to accomplish a similar sum by 60.

Bringing down the normal expense – In SIP, you encounter low normal cost. You put the equivalent settled dollar sum in similar speculation at customary interims over an all-encompassing timeframe. You are purchasing more offers of speculation when the offer cost is low. What's more, you are purchasing less offers when the offer cost is high. Also, it might result in you paying a lower normal cost for every offer.

The dollar-cost averaging technique does not attempt to time the market, or it may diminish the danger of putting a bigger sum in speculation at the wrong time.

Market timing insignificance – The past two passages reveal to you that SIP makes the market timing unimportant for you. The share trading system flightiness and instability frequently leads to obstruction for financial specialists like you. In SIP, you are totally free from the issue of wrong planning.

The SIP's Method of Capacity

A commonplace SIP involves month to month ventures over a time of 10, 15 or 25 years. You are, for the most, part permitted to begin your venture with a humble beginning. You do not have to coordinate responsibility for assets, or maybe you possess an enthusiasm for the arrangement of a trust. The arrangement trust contributes the speculator's normal installments, subsequent to deducting relevant expenses in offers of a shared store.

Things that you should clarify before putting resources into a SIP

i.   You should make certain things clear to yourself before going for SIP speculation.

ii.   You ought to be sure about proceeding to make installments for the term of the arrangement. Withdrawal midway will result, in all likelihood, profit, except if you are qualified for a full discount.

iii. Check the expenses charged by the arrangement. Additionally, check the conditions under which the arrangement postpones or lessens certain charges.

iv.   Study the arrangement's venture targets. Study the dangers of putting resources into the arrangement. Furthermore, check whether you are all right with them.

v.   Check your statutory rights to a discount on the off chance that you drop your arrangement.

401(k) and 403(b) Plans

If your employer offers a workplace-sponsored retirement plan such as a 401(k) or 403(b)), enroll in it as soon as you can. Essentially, that is a bonus that you should take advantage of because your employer will match your contribution dollar for dollar up to a certain percentage of gross income. Enroll in the plan and invest automatically during each bi-weekly pay period. In fact, many workplace retirement plans match dollar-for-dollar what you save, up to 6% of gross income in many cases. For example, if your gross income is $2,000.00 a pay period, you can invest up to 6% (or $120.00) a pay period, and your company will match the amount.

Your employer will typically offer a list of mutual funds available for selection in the prospectus that is provided by the company managing the mutual funds. Look at each mutual fund in the prospectus to determine the best rates of returns and expense ratios. Diversify your money among the best funds available or those that suit your needs.

The Powers of Compounding Money

Also, understand the powers of compounding money. Depending upon the rate of return and time (e.g., years) that you have to invest, your money can grow significantly. For example, if you start today with $10,000.00, and the money that you invest compounds at a rate of 5% a year, in twenty years you will have around $25,000.00. But since 5% is a conservative return, imagine the following scenarios:

If you start today with $10,000.00, and the money that you invest compounds at a rate of 10% a year, in twenty years you will have around $61,000.00.

If you start today with $10,000.00, and the money that you invest compounds at a rate of 15% a year, in twenty years you will have around $142,000.00.

If you start today with $10,000.00, and the money that you invest compounds at a rate of 20% a year, in twenty years you will have around $319,000.00!

Or if you start today with $10,000.00, and the money that you invest compounds at a rate of 25% a year, in twenty years you will have around $693,000.00!

Or take an extreme example: if you start today with $10,000.00, and the money that you invest compounds at a rate of 50% a year, in forty years you will have around $73,715,548,806.27!

Note that the above scenarios assume no added money and capital and no taxes.

The Powers of Compounding Money II

How about if you add $500.00 a month, or $1,000.00 a month in addition to the $10,000.00 that you started out with? If you start today with $10,000.00, add $500.00 a month to invest and the money that you invest compounds at an annual rate of 10% a year, in twenty years you will have around $89,000.00.

If you start today with $10,000.00, add $500.00 a month to invest, and the money that you invest compounds at an annual rate of 15% a year, in twenty years you will have around $193,000.00.

If you start today with $10,000.00, add $500.00 a month to invest, and the money that you invest compounds at an annual rate of 20% a year, in twenty years you will have around $412,000.00.

Or if you start today with $10,000.00, add $500.00 a month to invest, and the money that you invest compounds at an annual rate of 25% a year, in twenty years you will have around $864,000.00.

Or take an extreme example: if you start today with $10,000.00, add $500.00 a month to invest, and the money that you invest compounds at an annual rate of 50% a year, in forty years you will have around $84,772,879,627.21.

Based on the scenarios above, some of the hypothetical outcomes are below if you add $1,000.00 a month:

If you start today with $10,000.00, add $1,000.00 a month to invest, and the money that you invest compounds at an annual rate of 10% a year, in twenty years you will have around $117,000.00.

If you start today with $10,000.00, add $1,000.00 a month to invest, and the money that you invest compounds at an annual rate of 15% a year, in twenty years you will have around $243,000.00.

If you start today with $10,000.00, add $1,000.00 a month to invest and the money that you invest compounds at an annual rate of 20% a year, in twenty years you will have around $505,000.00!

Or if you start today with $10,000.00, add $1,000.00 a month to invest and the money that you invest compounds at an annual rate of 25% a year, in twenty years you will have around $1,035,000.00!

Or take an extreme example: if you start today with $10,000.00, add $1,000.00 a month to invest, and the money that you invest compounds at an annual rate of 50% a year, in forty years you will have around $73,715,548,806.27!

Again, these scenarios assume no added money and capital and no taxes.

CHAPTER 8

Strategies Used by Mutual Fund Managers

The mutual fund manager chooses the assets where the fund will be invested. Therefore, an investor must know the fund manager's style before he invests his money because the investment style may not fit his risk-reward overall plan. An investment style is important in investing because it is connected to the risks and rewards of the portfolio. Styles can be mixed in order to optimize diversification and balance risks and rewards.

Bottom-Up or Top-Down Investing

A top-down strategy includes the selection of assets in a theme. For example, the economy is expected to grow significantly, the fund manager may decide to purchase shares of stocks in all sectors or he may decide to purchase shares in high technology and industrial sectors only because these shares are known to outperform the others when there's a strong economy. On the other side, suppose the economy is expected to go into recession; the fund manager may sell the fund's assets or buy shares in consumer and health care sectors.

A bottom-up strategy allows the fund manager to select stocks based on a company's strength. It doesn't take into consideration the economic expectations in the near future. A manager thoroughly researches the company before he invests in it. However, it can still happen that the company experiences a market plunge even if it is a strong company. Here is an illustration of this strategy:

Top-Down Investment Process

Economic Data & Cycle Analysis

Event Risk

Market Decision

Sector Analysis

Security Selection

Technical or Fundamental Analysis

Fundamental analysis includes the evaluation of the different factors affecting the performance of the investment. If it's a stock, the fund manager has to go through the financial information of the company. He may initiate a meeting with the company's competitors, customers, suppliers, employees, and executives. He needs to analyze the company in order to find out the causes of its growth.

Technical analysis, on the other hand, includes the selection of assets based on previous trading patterns. Basically, the fund manager looks at the price of the investment in these trends. A lot of fund managers prefer fundamental analysis because they are interested in the growth of the company. Investors, on the other hand, expect the net asset value of the fund to increase if the company grows. However, the fundamental analysis doesn't always bring about the great news. On some days, technical analysis explains the market movement. A good fund manager employs both technical and fundamental analyses.

Contrarian Investing

A contrarian manager selects assets which run contrary to market consensus. This means that he first determines what the consensus of the market is, then he bets on the opposite of it. In general, it is related to value investing. The fund manager buys undervalued assets. He uses statistics in determining which assets are undervalued. Over time, the value will beat growth in assets. Contrarian investing rewards investors. However, the fund manager must select the right assets at the correct time. If the market consensus is right, the fund loses.

Dividend Investing

A mutual fund manager focuses on companies which provide dividends. He prefers regular payouts from the company. The rationale here is that the fund receives regular income even though the stock price of the company decreases. However, there are experts who suspect that the share price of the company is overvalued if it issues dividends. In general, the fund manager is also careful in investing in companies with very high yields because these firms may be headed for market plunges and have outsized risks.

CHAPTER 9

Mutual Fund Taxation

The tax rules of various countries differ regarding mutual funds. You are advised to refer to your wealth advisor for the taxation rules in your country.

Usually, the mutual funds are taxed at par with the stocks. For example, in some countries, if you are selling your mutual funds after a period of one year, then you are not taxed on your profits. There are some types of mutual funds, which provide exemption from taxes, of the income, that is invested in these funds.

Every investor is concerned about lowering the taxes he's paying on his mutual funds. In order to do so, it is necessary for the investor to understand taxation first so that he can improve the returns from his mutual funds. Tax avoidance or minimization is possible in mutual funds. It is up to the investor to acquire knowledge of taxation basics in order to generate better portfolio returns.

First, the investor must understand asset allocation. He must learn to choose mutual funds which don't charge high taxes. Income from dividend and bond funds is taxable to him. If he doesn't want to pay taxes, he can opt for a tax-deferred account like an annuity, 401(k) or IRA.

Second, taxes can be minimized if the investor opts for a mutual fund with no or little taxes. These mutual funds are known to tax-efficient. An investor who wants to invest in a bond fund can buy shares of a mutual fund specializing in municipal bonds because the federal government doesn't collect taxes on income from municipal bonds.

Third, a mutual fund may receive dividends from stock companies it invests in. Most of these dividends are distributed to investors, who often opt to reinvest the amount to the fund. However, the investor may owe taxes from the transaction but such taxes may depend on the investor's income tax bracket and holding period of the shares.

Fourth, the 1099 forms are often sent to investors through the mail. If an investor has received them, it is better that he understands the forms so that he can learn if the taxes due can be avoided or minimized.

Fifth, the distribution of capital gains can affect investors. Capital gains can result from the fund manager's decision to sell the fund assets within a given year. In order to help its investors, the mutual fund company posts capital gain estimates as early as October. This way, the investor can plan how to deal with taxes he will have to pay.

Sixth, a lot of investors don't realize that they can avoid or minimize taxes on capital gains. They can offset the capital gains with losses they incur from their portfolio thereby reducing or eliminating taxes.

Seventh, managed mutual funds pay more taxes because they have higher turnover. On the other hand, an exchange-traded fund or index fund may be considered by the investor if he wants to minimize his taxes.

Mutual Fund Regulations

Mutual funds are one of the most popular and efficient of all investment options. This can be attributed to its reputation for honesty, integrity and fairness. This reputation is built on a system that is designed to ensure that the funds operate in the best interest of their shareholders.

In addition, these funds are also governed by boards of directors, 40 percent of whom must be independent of the fund and who must act as advocates on behalf of the shareholders.

Most often, these funds exceed the legal requirement by maintaining a majority of independent directors on their boards.

The System Regulating Mutual Funds

Mutual funds are required by law to observe an extensive set of strict federal laws and regulations which are actively enforced and monitored by the regulating authority to ensure compliance.

The Security and Exchange Commission (SEC)

This is the main federal agency that is tasked with regulating mutual funds. The commission is responsible for monitoring the fund's compliance with the Investment Company Act of 1940, the chief federal statute governing mutual funds.

This act imposes restrictions both on mutual funds as well as on the investment advisers, principal underwriters, directors, officers, and employees that run the fund.

The SEC also monitors funds' compliance with other federal statutes like the Investment Advisers Act, the Security Exchange Act of 1934 and the Securities Act of 1933.

The SEC Division of Investment Management is responsible for overseeing and regulating funds; and also looking into changes to the securities laws that affect funds and other investment companies. Guided by the 1940 Act, SEC Division of Investment Management is tasked with the following:

- Working to prevent conflicts of interest in order to ensure that the funds are only serving the interests of their shareholders

- Maintaining strict standards of leveraging to prevent funds from taking undue risks with their assets

- Ensuring that funds maintain an effective self-governance system

- Requiring understandable and full disclosure to investors while working to eliminate fraud and abuse

- Analyzing laws together with regulations for the community and for SEC enforcement and inspection purposes

- Reviewing funds' required filings with the SEC

- Reviewing funds' enforcement matters

- Developing new rules and amendments to adopt a regulation to new circumstances

Office of Compliance Inspections and Examinations

Within the SEC is the Office of Compliance Inspections and Examinations (OCIE). This office performs a nationwide examination and inspection program for mutual funds and other investment programs.

This office inspects funds to ensure compliance with the 1940 Act as well as other securities laws, identify possible violations, and inform SEC of developments in the fund industry.

Office of Investor Education and Assistance (OIEA)

This is yet another office under the SEC. This office serves individual investors directly, ensuring that their concerns are reported to the SEC and considered when the agency is taking action.

You can contact this office for questions, complaints, and an informal resolution of disputes arising from your investment. This office also publishes educational materials on various investing topics. You can get these materials by contacting the SEC.

Other Regulating Agencies and Bodies

Department of Labor

The Department of Labor's Employee Benefits Security Administration (EBSA) ensures the protection of the integrity of pension plans, such as 401(k), as well as plans that mutual funds provide services to. EBSA assists workers in accessing the information they need to protect their benefit rights while enforcing the relevant provisions of federal pension laws.

NASD Regulation, Inc.

This body regulates the entire security industry, including mutual funds, according to 1930s federal laws that allow for the establishment of "self-regulatory" organizations under the oversight of the SEC. As a result, every mutual fund communication is required by law to comply with NASD rules and regulations.

Internal Revenue Service (IRS)

The IRS does not have any direct oversight on mutual funds. However, its regulations and decisions affect how mutual funds conduct their business and can thus impact your fund's investment through its tax policies.

The Fund Directors

Every mutual fund is governed by a board of directors that work to ensure that the fund management serves the best interest of the shareholders while running the fund. The law holds these directors to a very high standard.

As such, these directors are expected to exercise the care that a reasonably prudent person would take with his own money. They should obtain adequate information, practice sound judgment, approve policies and procedures, and undertake oversights while reviewing the performance of investment managers and other entities that are serving the fund.

Mutual funds make investments and savings fairly simple, affordable, and accessible. The greatest advantages of mutual funds include diversification, professional management, liquidity, variety, convenience, affordability, and ease of record keeping, as well as strict federal regulation and full disclosure. However, before investing in any fund, you need to understand its ins and outs as well as what is in it for you.

Mutual Fund Data

Nowadays, mutual fund data is very easy to find and read. Previously, the main source of mutual fund tables used to be the newspapers, but now this information is easily available online on websites which provide significantly more data. Yahoo Finance, MSN Money and all of the major mutual fund companies provide robust websites filled with fund information. Also, fund fact sheets and a copy of the fund's prospectus are available on most fund company websites.

The information available on websites is well categorized. The basic details provided include fund name, net asset value, price change, previous close price, year-to-date return, net assets, and yield. Detailed information like historical prices, headline news, fund holdings, ratings, etc., along with different duration graphs are also available on websites. Thus, all this information, analysis reports, can be very helpful for investors to make the decisions which suit their respective needs and how they plan to invest.

Mutual Fund Performance

Lots of mutual fund ads quote their amazingly high one-year rates of return. However, when long term performances are reviewed, it is found that three-year performance is lower, and the five-year is yet even lower. This is not atypical, especially because when the funds list the various year performances, they generally show averages which basically camouflage the years of poor performances.

It should be noted that performance is a very relative issue. Knowing the fund's performance is just part of the information. If the fund in the example was judged against its appropriate benchmark index, a whole new layer of information would be added to the evaluation. If the index returned 50% for 2012, the 34.5% from the fund would not look quite so good. On the other hand, if the index delivered results of 20%, 5%, and 2% for the respective one, three, and five-year periods, then the fund's results look rather fine indeed.

To add another layer of information to the evaluation, one can consider a fund's performance against its peer group as well as against its index. If other funds that invest with a similar mandate had similar performance, this data point tells us that the fund is in line with its peers. If the fund outperformed its peers and benchmark, its results would be impressive indeed.

Looking at any one piece of information in isolation only tells a small portion of the story. Consider the comparison of a fund against its peers. If the fund sits in the top slot over each of the comparison periods, it is likely to be a solid performer. If it sits at the bottom, it may be even worse than perceived, as peer group comparisons only capture the results from existing funds. Many fund companies are in the habit of closing their worst performers. When the "losers" are purged from their respective categories, their statistical records are no longer included in the category performance data. This makes the category averages creep higher than they would have if the losers were still in the mix. This is better known as survivorship bias.

To develop the best possible picture of a fund's performance results, as many data points as possible should be considered. Long-term investors should focus on long-term results, keeping in mind that even the best performing funds have bad years from time to time.

Comparison between Exchange Trade and Mutual Funds

Despite the fact that this guide is not based on ETFs, well known as exchange traded funds, it is vital to briefly highlight ETFs, especially with reference to the differences as distinguished to mutual funds. This is because they go hand in hand. Well, the exchange trade funds are like the mutual funds, since both of them bundle together securities to offer investors varied portfolios. Up to three thousand different securities can form a fund. However, the two types of investment are marked by substantial variances.

When it comes to trading, the exchange trade operates during the day. On the other hand, the mutual funds perform their operations at a closing of a net asset of values.

The expenses involved in the operation of exchange trade funds are low. As for mutual funds, such expenses do vary.

On the line of creating and redeeming shares, the exchange trade funds do so with in-kind transactions which are not considered as sales, hence no taxable events. On the other hand, redemptions create tax events in mutual funds.

The exchange trade funds don't have minimum investments, while such investments exist in mutual funds.

When we talk of exchange trade funds, there is no such a thing as sales load while mutual funds have such.

As for the exchange trade funds, they are tax efficient, while mutual funds lacks this.

Scenarios on when to Bid Goodbye to Mutual Funds

While there are many investment consultants, some by profession, some self-professed, who suggest when to invest in a particular avenue, there is a certain paucity of people who talk about when to exit. People looking to invest get in many options and mutual funds happen to be one such preferred destination for people who want more returns than their fixed deposits would earn them. It's also a preferred option for the people who are circumspect about investing into stocks directly and believe that mutual funds can manage risks and funds better than they could.

The recent crash has several lessons for the investor but will not drive them away from the mutual funds in the wake of falling returns because they still are among the best investment avenues available to them. The primary of the lessons learned is not to chase returns. One of the biggest flaws in the process of investing is to chase the performance of funds alone. While they do give an indication of how well a fund can perform, they remain just expressive. Take, for example, the case of several equity funds that were riding sky-high between October 1999 and March 2000. The Alliance Equity Fund posted absolute returns of 168 percent between October 1, 1999 and March 7, 2000. Birla Advantage posted 125 gains and ING Growth Fund posted mind-boggling returns of 193 percent during the same period. The recommendation by the consultants remained to "buy." However, investors who chased the returns of these schemes have learned the bitter and eternal truth that "what goes up must come down" the hard way. These funds have posted negative returns of 64 percent, 61 percent, and 82 percent respectively since peaking on the same day, March 7, 2000. And so, while chasing hot funds might be a good idea in a market that has started to rise, it certainly is a sure recipe to doom in a peaking market. The only people to have gained from investing in these schemes were those who exited while it was still profitable.

The others did not know when to exit, so we are just trying to put forward some situations when the investor should consider withdrawing their investments from the funds.

The fund is not performing

This reason for selling, although valid in certain conditions, is where most investors make a mistake. When calculating performance, one shouldn't look at too short a period and make a mistake by comparing apples to oranges.

It is important to base the resolution on virtual performance and not absolute performance. When one fund is down 5% while other funds (or the market in general) are up 10%, it is very tempting to switch over to what is "hot." Chasing performance is the best way to shoot oneself in the foot, as we just discussed above.

When studying relative performance, one should look at his fund and compare it to its peers. However, comparisons should be drawn between parallels and so equity funds cannot and should not be compared with debt funds. When choosing a benchmark, one must select funds in the same category. If one's fund was down 2% and the average equity fund was down 4%, then there is no good enough reason to sell. One should compare the returns posted by his fund with that of the peers across various horizons such as 1-year, 3-year, and above. A short-term view can often lead to committing something bad as it doesn't present the full picture. If it has underperformed the average of its peers in all cases, then it sure is one of the better reasons to exit from the fund.

A change in life stage

Investments are made with a certain objective in mind, and life stages are often a determining factor of what a person needs. A young man can afford to take more risks than a person nearing his retirement. In such cases, it pays to withdraw money from the equity investments made earlier and put them in safer, more conservative debt funds that offer stable returns without compromising on risk. So a change in life phases would be a motive to consider switching into a fund that matches one's needs. As one nears retirement, one might want to consider more conservative funds. If one gets married, one might need to compromise one's risk tolerance and desired returns with that of the spouse. This could trigger the need to exit.

A major change in any basic attribute of the fund

When the fund changes any basic attribute as mentioned by it in its offer documents, the investors have a choice of getting out of it. Even SEBI has provided for an exit route being made available to the investors. Changes like a change in Asset Management Company, investment style of fund, or change of structure (say from closed-end to open-end etc.) are good enough reasons for an investor to consider switching or exiting from it as they are certainly likely to affect the fund in a major way.

The fund doesn't comply with its objective

One of the important parameters in the selection of the fund is the alignment of the risk profiles of the investor and fund. The objective of the fund says a lot about how the fund plans to invest. If the objective is not being met, it is one of the reasons worth considering to quite. For example, the three funds discussed above, Alliance Equity, Birla Advantage, and ING Growth all claim to be diversified equity funds, yet they had huge exposures to select ICE sector scrip that not only added volatility that is expected out of diversified funds but also, in a way, went against their stated objectives.

The Fund's Expense Ratio Rises

A small rise in an expense ratio is not a big deal, however a significant rise can result in substantial reduction of yields, so it would be better to exit the fund. In the case of bond funds or money market funds, it is highly unlikely that the fund can increase its returns enough to justify an increase in the fund's expenses.

The Fund Manager Has Changed

A simple change of fund managers in itself is not enough reason to sell a fund on a short-term basis. If it is a passively managed fund (index fund), then one has little to no reason to worry. However, if it is an actively managed fund, then one must keep his or her eyes open to the new manager. Observing the styles, stock picking, and risks undertaken by the new manager is important, for it discloses a lot about how the fund might fare in the future. If satisfied, one will have no reason to complain later, but the process needs time, so an investor has to observe the fund manager for some time before one makes a decision.

Enough has been earned

However, nothing is as important as to rein in the horses in time. The primary principle behind the safety of investment is to take risks that can be tolerated. The principle also is specific to the expectations that the investor must have from any investment. Just as it is important to set realistic targets that one hopes to achieve from the investment, it is also important to exit when a target has been achieved as expected. irrespective of the fact that it might be generating better returns in the short-term. Waiting longer might not prove beneficial, as one may not be lucky all the time. Equity investments are volatile, and it doesn't take long for the moods in the markets to swing either way. So, it would only be wise to move out when the going is still good. Otherwise, the investor's sanguine attitude of generating even higher returns than the fund generated in its peak days, would be cursing themselves for not exiting.

The above list is certainly not exhaustive and individuals will have other better reasons to quit as well. It's just that most don't know when to apply, so these would come in handy.

How to Manage Portfolios

In mutual fund portfolio management, there are mainly three parameters. Those are (1) Time duration (2) Risk (3) Amount (4) Portfolio concentration.

Those parameters also can be subdivided as follows:

Time Duration:

For portfolio management, you need to understand the time duration. That means for how long you can be invested. It looks simple, but it is not so simple. There are some parameters which affect your investment tenure. Those are as follows.

Dependency: The first parameter in the time duration is the dependency. In simple words, you need to understand how much you depend on the money that you invest in a mutual fund. If your dependency is high and you can't keep this money invested for a long term, then the performance of your investment may not be as good as you expected.

Emergency fund: The next factor you need to comprehend is emergency fund. Sometimes we see the market is so favorable to invest in being influenced by friends or some people threfore we invest all our emergency money in a mutual fund. An emergency fund is for a medical emergency or something of that nature. When all is good, we forget and invest all the money. But when an emergency comes, we withdraw money with no option left to us. At that time, the market may be down, which can cause you a loss also.

Withdrawal time: During mutual fund investments, we first focus on withdrawal time. How much time do we have before withdrawing money from the fund? If we have a long period we can choose equity to get the advantage of high return, if we have less time we can invest in debt, and if we have an average time of nearly 5 years we can choose a balanced fund.

Risk

Before any mutual fund investments, we need to understand how much risk we can take according to our age. If we play too risky and aggressive without understanding how much risk we can take, that may lead to a capital loss. And if we play it too safe, we may not create adequate wealth at the end of the day.

Debt: As we get older, we get shorter investment time. So we should choose debt oriented investment. Debt-oriented investments are not too risky. At an older age, generally we try to play it safe. So debt oriented investment is the best option at an older age.

Equity: At a younger age, you risk-taking ability is greater, and we can take more risk. We can play aggressively to create wealth for our future. The equity market is riskier, so it gives more return. So, at a younger age, we should try to invest in equity-oriented funds.

Amount

According to the investment amount and market conditions, we should choose the investment amount option.

Lump-sum: Sometimes we get confused about the investment amount option. We see everyone talking about how a SIP investment is good. But lump-sum investments are also not bad. If you are a consist investor, and if you keep a close eye on two indexes called Sensex and nifty, you will see the market fall and market rise. As days go on your investment experience will increase, and then you can approximately time the market. You can invest in a lump-sum when the market falls. But for that, you need to continuously study those two indexes. If you follow those two indexes, you will find that market timing is not so difficult in case of mutual fund lump-sum investment.

SIP: If we start our investment journey with small money, SIP is the best solution. SIP is the best solution for beginners. They do not understand the market well and less skill is required.

Portfolio Concentration

In portfolio management, understanding a portfolio concentration is very important. If we don't understand portfolio concentrations, we may not handle portfolios actively. Here portfolio concentration means a combined portfolio of the total fund or asset you are holding.

Aggressive or wealth creation: If the total Portfolio contains a maximum percentage of equity investment, this can be called an aggressive portfolio. It is desirable for wealth creation for a young investor.

Balanced or consolidate: If the overall portfolio contains a nearly equal distribution of debt and equity, then this is called a balanced portfolio. This type of portfolio is best when investment tenure is mid-range.

Wealth protection: If overall the portfolio contains maximum debt, this type of portfolio is called wealth protection. This type of portfolio is best for an older investor during retirement. Here the risk is very low compared to the return.

CHAPTER 10

Performance Measures of Mutual Fund

With a plethora of structures to select from, the retail investor faces problems in selecting funds. Factors such as investment strategy and management style are qualitative, but the fund's record is an important indicator, too. Though past performance alone cannot be indicative of future performance, it is, frankly, the only quantitative way to judge how good a fund is at present. Therefore, there is a need to analyze the previous performance relating to distinct mutual funds correctly.

Worldwide, good mutual fund companies are known by their AMCs, and this fame is directly linked to their superior stock selection skills. For mutual funds to grow, AMCs must be held accountable for their selection of stocks. In other words, there must be some performance indicator that will reveal the quality of stock selection of various AMCs.

Return alone should not be considered as the basis of measurement of the performance of a mutual fund scheme, it should also include the risk taken by the fund manager, because different funds will have different levels of risk attached to them. The risk associated with a fund, in a general, can be defined as variability or fluctuations in the returns generated by it. The higher the fluctuations in the returns of a fund during a given period, the higher will be the risk associated with it. These fluctuations in the returns generated by a fund are resultant of two guiding forces. First, general market fluctuations, which affect all the securities present in the market called market risk or systematic risk, and second, fluctuations due to specific securities present in the portfolio of the fund, called unsystematic risk. The total risk of a specific fund is the total of these two and is measured in terms of the standard deviation of returns of the fund. Systematic risk, on the other hand, is measured in terms of beta, which represents fluctuations in the NAV of the fund vis-à-vis the market. The more responsive the NAV of a mutual fund is to the changes in the market, the higher will be its beta. Beta is calculated by relating the returns on a mutual fund with the returns in the market. While unsystematic risk can be diversified through investments in a number of instruments, systematic risk cannot. By using the risk-return relationship, we try to assess the competitive strength of the mutual funds vis-à-vis one another in a better way.

In order to determine the risk-adjusted returns of investment portfolios, several eminent authors have worked to develop composite performance indices to evaluate a portfolio by comparing alternative portfolios within a particular risk class. The most important and widely used measures of performance are:

- The Sharpe Measure

- Treynor Measure

- Jenson Model

- Fama Model

The Sharpe Measure

To evaluate the performance of mutual funds in this model, the analysis of a fund is assessed on the basis of Sharpe Ratio. It is the returns ratio produced by the fund over and above the risk-free rate of return and total risk associated with it. In relation to Sharpe, it is the total risk of the fund where the investors put their concentration on. Therefore, this performance measure evaluates funds basing on reward per unit involved in the total risk. It is simplified as follows:

(Si)Sharpe index $= (Ri - Rf)/Si$

Where, Si is the fund's standard deviation.

To analyze the idea, a high and positive Sharpe Ratio implies superior risk-adjusted performance of a fund, while a low and negative Sharpe Ratio is an implication of negative performance.

Treynor Measure

In this analysis, performance measure evaluates the funds based on Treynor's Index, where the index stands for return ratio produced by the fund over and above risk-free return rates during a given period and systematic risk associated with it (beta). The idea is simplified as follows:

(Ti) Treynor's Index = (Ri - Rf)/Bi.

Where, Ri stands for return on the fund, Rf stands for risk-free return rate,

and Bi stands for beta of the fund.

A high and positive Treynor's Index implies superior risk-adjusted performance of a fund, while a low and negative Treynor's Index is an implication of negative performance.

Jenson Model

It is also referred to as the differential return method. In this model, it proposes another adjusted risk performance measure. This measure, implemented by Michael Jenson, involves evaluation of the returns generated by the funds vs. the returns expected out of the fund given the level of its systematic risk. The surplus between the two returns is known as alpha, which measures the performance of a fund as compared with the actual returns over the period. The required return of a fund at a given risk level (Bi) is simplified as follows:

$Ri = Rf + Bi (Rm-Rf)$ Where Rm stands for the average market return during the specific period. After the calculations, alpha can be obtained by subtracting the required return from the actual return of the fund.

Higher alpha implies a superior performance of the fund and vice versa.

Fama Model

The Eugene Fama criteria is an addition to the Jenson model. It compares the performance, measured in terms of returns, of a fund with the required return commensurate, with the total risk associated with it. The difference between these two is taken as a measure of the performance of the fund and is called net selectivity.

The net selectivity represents the stock selection skill of the fund manager, as it is the excess return over and above the return required to compensate for the total risk taken by the fund manager. A higher value of which indicates that the fund manager has earned returns well above the return commensurate with the level of risk taken by him.

Required return can be calculated as: $Ri = Rf + Si/Sm*(Rm-Rf)$

Where Sm is a standard deviation of market returns. The net selectivity is then calculated by subtracting this required return from the actual return of the fund.

Among the above performance measures, two models, namely, Treynor measure and Jenson model, use systematic risk based on the premise that the unsystematic risk is diversifiable. These models are suitable for big investors such as the one involved in institutional, with high risk-taking capacities, as they do not face paucity of funds and can invest in a number of options to dilute some risks. For them, a portfolio can be spread across a number of stocks and sectors. However, the Sharpe measure and Fama model that considers the entire risk associated with fund is suitable for small investors, as the ordinary investor lacks the necessary skill and resources to diversify. Moreover, the selection of the fund on the basis of superior stock selection ability of the fund manager will also help in safeguarding the money invested to a great extent. The investment in funds that have generated big returns at higher levels of risks leaves the money all the more prone to risks of all kinds that may exceed the individual investor's risk appetite.

Conclusion

Congratulations for reaching the end of everything you need to know about mutual funds on the stock market and what you can do to begin partaking in the field yourself. I know when you are first starting, it seems scary, or that you aren't going to make money doing it, but trust me on this.

Follow the outlined rules and guidelines I have set up and work with the system. The more you work with the rules of the trade, the better off things end up, and the more profit you bring home.

As with any part of the market, this is going to require its own set of practice and devotion, but you'll get it. Dedicate practice and ambition, and in no time at all you will have it down. I know because I've done it, and I have helped countless other people get started, too.

Now it's your turn. Don't give up, make mutual funds the next thing to do on your list, and dedicate the time and effort you need to make it happen. There is no end to the things you can do on the market when you know how, and it's my goal to ensure that you do.

Take the information here and use it to your advantage. Don't be that person who is always watching and gathering information but who never actually gets out there or does anything with the information that they gather. When you are in the stock market, you have to make a move, or nothing is ever going to happen for you.

I know you have what it takes to be an excellent investor, and I want to give you the tools you need to get out there and diversify your portfolio with confidence. All you require is a little drive in the right direction, and you are only going to gain momentum from there.

You know you want to climb to the top, and you'll get there, one step at a time.

Made in the USA
Monee, IL
17 May 2020